Case Studies

KV-476-164

Schools Council Environmental Studies Project

Rupert Hart-Davis Educational Publications   London

Granada Publishing Limited
First published in Great Britain 1972
by Rupert Hart-Davis Educational Publications Ltd
3 Upper James Street W1R 4BP

ISBN 0 247 54440 X ⌐ 0048468

Photoset by Keyspools Ltd, Golborne, Lancs.
Printed by C. Tinling & Co. Ltd, London and Prescot

Case Studies

The Schools Council Environmental Studies Project team have prepared four books to illustrate their approach with children of the 5 to 13 age range:

A Teacher's Guide
Case Studies
Starting from Maps
Starting from Rocks

The members of the Project:
Melville Harris, director
Meurig Evans, deputy director
Gwenallt Rees
Douglas Myers
Stephen Moore, evaluator

This book was edited
by Melville Harris and
Meurig Evans

Contents

Ham Lane   9

The River   22

A Village Transect   28

A Village Survey   40

The Cave   45

Working with Less Able Children   53

Mud   58

Our Homes   65

The Crossroads   74

The Castle   83

Environmental Studies and the Handicapped Child   89

Environmental Studies in a Secondary Special
Education Department   95

A Study in an Urban Setting   104

Using the Environment in a Rural Comprehensive School   113

Preface

The Case Studies in this volume illustrate the work undertaken in schools, in the field of Environmental Studies, by children in the age range 5–13 years. They have been selected from a large number of studies produced by schools participating in the Schools Council Project on Environmental Studies.

The studies indicate the different aims of an environmental studies approach at various stages in a child's school life. At the infant stage the locality is seen to be used to advance the children's development in language and mathematics. The junior school studies broaden and deepen, to involve not only the language and mathematics skills but also the study and social skills which are considered the core activities of this approach. At secondary level the further development of skills and the growing awareness for some children of subject specialisations are illustrated. Through all the studies the interest and enjoyment of children and teachers involved in work of this type is apparent.

Careful study and comparison of the case studies will emphasise the variations in the conditions under which they were produced. Examples can be seen, at infant, junior and secondary school level, of studies involving city and country sites with children of different abilities. The particular physical and cultural environments vary greatly, but in each case a common denominator of active enquiry aimed at developing study and communication skills and providing stimulating experiences is evident.

This active enquiry has, in some instances, been carried out by children and teachers who were relatively inexperienced in using this approach. Consequently, a considerable degree of direction by the teacher is evident throughout some of these studies. Other examples show how teachers with greater experience and self-confidence utilise less direction of the work and permit a broadening of the study. Also, examples of a further stage of development, where both children and teacher are experienced in the approach, are included. At this stage emerges the teacher's role of adviser and consultant, with the children playing a large part in the organisation of the study.

Comparison of studies conducted with children of similar ages in streamed and mixed ability classes shows the differences in approaches and the nature of work produced. Such comparisons emphasise the fact that environmental studies is an approach to the intellectual and social development of children not an exercise for the description of the environment. It is a further tool for teachers who can modify its use according to the needs of their children.

It must be emphasised that these studies, written by the teachers who developed them with their children, originated as part of the normal activities of the school and not for publication. Indeed, it is doubtful if anyone approaching the work with publication in mind could develop the spontaneity so evident in many of these studies. The volume is available through the readiness of the individual teachers who, amid all the pressures of work, were prepared to record their thoughts on situations and events within their schools. The editors wish to place on record their gratitude for this ready co-operation.

M. I. HARRIS & R. M. EVANS

Ham Lane

Ham Lane is a road at the eastern end of a rapidly growing seaside village. Part of it runs north to south and the school is situated at the southern end. The part we studied most closely was the quarter of a mile or so from the caravan site in Ham Manor Woods to a main road.

Years ago the lane was but a lane with beautiful old Ham Manor nestling in the trees at the bottom. Gradually it has changed. A large housing estate – council and Ministry of Defence property – has been built to the west; our school is to the east. A new Secondary Modern school is above us and more housing development below. Until January 1969 the top part of the lane was still very narrow and quite a bottleneck for all the traffic using it. It was also dangerous for our infants to walk up as there was only a very narrow pavement.

The County Council decided to widen the road. Diversion signs and *Slow, Men at Work* road signs blossomed overnight. Workmen, pneumatic drills, bulldozers, picks and shovels all started to make their impression on the Lane.

School started. Children almost made themselves late by standing watching the busy men. Until now I had not been very conscious of all the activity, but on the third day of term I was made sharply aware of something else: mud on the floor. Masses of it! Following the trail I came to the school gate. The footsteps – thick, brown, muddy footsteps – vanished into the distance up the Lane.

'Where on earth is all this mud coming from?'

'Up Ham Lane!'

'Well, you mustn't walk on the banks, keep to the pavement.'

'They're digging up the road and the pavement and the bank and...' So it all began.

I thought that reclaiming the children's interest after the Christmas holiday would follow the normal pattern, but here they were buzzing with excitement, and the term only three days old! Quick, I thought, jump in now! It was not planned at all. We all 'jumped in' together.

That Friday we arranged our first visit, accompanied by the Nursery Assistant.

The top half of the lane was completely closed and even pedestrians were frowned upon, but up we went.

It was a cloudy day; some of the workmen were in their hut

and the others were leaning on their picks and pneumatic drills. They stared at us and the children stared at them. 'This is a fine start', I thought. So I began to play my part: 'Look at this.' 'What is that?' 'Don't do that.' The men still stared. Perhaps they had seen Joyce Grenfell and were fascinated by a 'real one'. Blue with cold I decided to call it all off. At that one of the children remarked: 'Can't see much can we? Why don't they do something?' Turning a shade pink I muttered something about how interesting it all was and followed them back to school. 'The quickest study I've ever done,' I thought as we turned in at the gate – all over in a quarter of an hour. That was the lull before the storm, or the charging of the batteries, whichever way you like to look at it. A discussion followed; questions asked and answered ended with a promise that we would go up again and see if we could see any difference. If only those workmen had realised what was going on! Here breathing down their necks were thirty would-be foremen all demanding action.

So it was planned to have a class book to put all our Ham Lane observations in.

The children, daily, brought fresh news of what was going on. It was a fortnight later when we all visited again. This time it was trying to snow. The men saw us coming and the show was really impressive. The noise was terrible and we were nearly choked by the fumes from the air compression unit. Jane's Uncle Evan was the foreman and he told us what was going on.

Water pipes, drain pipes and electricity cables were to be laid in the huge trench the men were digging and afterwards a six foot wide pavement on the top. To gain all this information I had to ask the chief driller to stop for a little rest, which he did gladly. The well-established trees down one side of the Lane were apparently old and rotten and they all had to come down so on the way back to school we counted them – lovingly – seeing them perhaps for the first time. There were eighteen.

Ham Lane now began to be far more than an interesting feature to be studied, it was our whole life. We started to make books for everything:
(a) Ham Lane Road Works
(b) Mathematics and Ham Lane
(c) Looking at Nature in Ham Lane
(d) People who work in Ham Lane.

Some children wanted their own Ham Lane work books, which were duly produced.

Many visits followed, producing a vast quantity of written work and also some colourful paintings which were mounted with captions so that they made an explanatory wall story of what was going on.

The highlight of one visit was the huge yellow monster which had recently appeared on the scene. This, Uncle Evan told us, was a brand new hydraulic road roller and it had cost over £4,000. It was so new and shiny. It just lay there in regal splendour dominating the scene. A small grey roller was further down the road. This they clambered over until Uncle Evan asked if David would like to drive it. He would. In he clambered and he waved to the crowd. At that moment the roller started off, much to David's surprise. Up and down he went. Here he was, a six-year-old infant turned roadman. He was thrilled by it all and everyone else was very envious. Later Janette painted a lovely picture of it. Months afterwards I happened to have a letter from David's mother about something else and she mentioned his marvellous ride and how he would remember it all his life. Even now, seven months afterwards, David still regards it as the highlight of his infant school life.

We watched loads of gravel arrive; we watched them tipped. We ran up the road especially to see a cement mixing tanker in action. Malcolm, of course, knew 'Edgar, the gravel'. Malcolm seemed to know them all.

Peter painted a picture of a gravel lorry arriving with its load. A little man was handing something to the driver.

'What's that, Peter?'

'A nice cup of tea,' he replied.

No doubt it would have been well received as we were still in the middle of winter.

The middle of February arrived. The road works were progressing slowly and rather repetitively and I wondered if we should soon finish our project. Then it happened. February 10th I think it was.

The field to the south of our school grounds had always been just a field. We saw it clearly from our large classroom windows. Cows wandered there and the occasional tractor trundled through. On this day a strange lorry arrived. There were several men and large bits of wood. Full of excitement we dashed out to see what was up: for this field was in Ham Lane and Ham Lane belonged to us (for a few months anyway). Part of the hedge had been ripped away to allow the lorry in. The field was terribly wet and the imprints of the cows' hooves were full of water. I thought quickly of parental reaction if all the children arrived home up to their eyes in mud. I decided to let four children, two boys and two girls, go across the middle of the field to see what was going on. Four children to clean is better than thirty. Nicola, Jane, Peter and Andrew squelched their way over to where the men were busy erecting a wooden hut. Ten minutes later they made the return journey.

'What are they doing?' clamoured the children.

We gathered that the field had been sold and that 'they' were going to build some houses there. 'They've started one already,' volunteered Andrew. I had to put him right on that score for surely this was the workmen's rest hut. I asked what it was like inside. When I heard the answer I wondered whether or not I had been wise sending these four innocents on this fact finding mission.

'Inside on the walls there are lots and lots of pictures of ladies and they haven't got any ...'

'Oh, very interesting,' I interrupted quickly. 'How nice. Time to go back to school now.'

We had now a new boost to our enthusiasm. Much discussion followed about new houses generally and we thought about all the different men and materials we would see on the site. For several days it was hard to get the children to do any recorded work. I had said: 'Now keep your eyes open and every time you see something new and interesting in the field — write it down.' This was all very well until I realised that they all had their eyes glued on the windows, looking and waiting.

The surveyors came. Red and white poles appeared all over the field. We were intrigued with the theodolite, only to be told later that it was not a theodolite but a dumpy level. The corners of the houses were pegged out and the roads were marked.

Comparative peace descended on us for a week. Nothing was happening now in the field. The road works were almost completed and the trees started to fall.

Much mud found its way into the classroom again. The roots

of the trees were deeply embedded in the earth and when they were dug out the road once again was a mud bath.

Felling trees is a hazardous occupation at the best of times but with infants in the way it would be worse. For this reason we kept our distance. We saw the cable put round the tree trunk and the woodman used an electric saw to cut through the trunk, then the crane pulled it across the road. The lorry-crane was old and it kept breaking down. We learnt that the trees were being stripped of the branches and then sent to the sawmills where they would eventually be turned into packing cases.

Back at school we had a slight diversion on trees and sawmills and a little about the industry in Canada. This interested the children but they were more interested in what was going to be in the packing cases and where they would go.

The lumberjack was very pleasant with the children and he promised he would cut them a special slice across the trunk of the next tree. I was pleased about this, thinking of the nature study I could introduce, and they were delighted because they would see it all happening.

Half term and the snow. It was so deep, Ham Lane was transformed. To get into school you had to negotiate deep drifts and, of course, the trees lying under them. Very few children arrived on those two days. The ones that did come continued with Ham Lane, weighing bricks, measuring bricks, playing with sand, cement and gravel.

When the snow melted an army of scrapers arrived on the building site. They worked continuously, pushing earth here and there. One huge pile of earth was formed and the children still refer to that as the dump. The yellow scrapers were like busy ants pushing their way up and down it all day. The noise was terrible. One thing all the children could do was draw a scraper. Peter and Christopher are happy children but learn more slowly than the others. Now, however, they drew the best mechanical diggers in the class and their daily news, once non-existent, was 'I played down the dumps last night'. This project really sparked them off. Now every child in the class is capable of writing on his own.

We added a new book to our collection: 'We discover the way to build houses'. Nicola is having a house built at the moment so she was very well informed as to what was going to happen next. The scrapers still worked and the field changed its appearance.

The trees disappeared overnight and we saw neither the lumberjack nor our piece of trunk. Andrew was very disappointed. We all were. He wrote a plaintive little piece for the book: '. . . and the man promist he would give us a bit, he promist, he really did.'

We continued to learn about how to build houses; all about the bricks, the glazier, the electrician, the plumber, the tiler, etc., but still no houses appeared.

At this stage of the year I always introduced a shop for the practical use of money. It was usually a cake shop, with cakes made with flour and salt pastry. This keeps well and looks clean and inviting for some weeks.

This year I could not see how I could get them to accept a cake shop when they were more interested in sand, gravel and bricks. I put it to the children. A few suggestions followed like a 'sweet shop', 'an ice cream shop', and then a voice called out 'a builder's shop'. There was the answer — Ham Lane Builders' Merchants was born (fig. 1).

We made it all up and opened the shop that week. Real money was in the bank and Peter and Diane were appointed as bankers. Children respect real money and I have found that they might as well learn with the real thing as cardboard imitation. It need never be lost if it is checked at the end of each session. I made out shopping cards ranging from 'What can I buy for $1\frac{1}{2}$ new pence?' to 'I want to build a wall, I have $12\frac{1}{2}$ new pence.' They learnt to use it well. Grace was a shy little girl and she could not bring herself to shop so I asked Peter to take her shopping with him. I watched them go. Luckily as they moved from bank to shop I was near enough to hear what was going on. Grace clutched a 'What can I buy for $2\frac{1}{2}$ new pence?' card in her hand along with $2\frac{1}{2}$ new pence. She stood and looked. Peter tried to tempt her to this and that and then he said: 'How do you feel about a bag of sand?'

'All right,' murmured Grace.

'Good,' said Peter, 'that'll be 1 new pence.'

It was so comical. I wondered how Grace really felt about a bag of sand. Anyway she came away with her sand, putty and two nails, and after that she managed the expedition on her own.

Another class book was made 'All about our Shop'. There are some delightful stories in it about how the children made the bricks, cement, putty and how they bagged sand and gravel and cut up wood. Throughout the term the shop was in constant use and it was very gratifying to find the assignments cards so well worn and the plastic bags (full of sand, gravel or cement) so well patched. Apparently shopping for nails and a bag of sand at the same time usually meant a hole in the bag and sand on the floor (fig. 2).

On the site the work continued slowly. The roads were defined, and drains were laid. At last they started to dig the footings. They had started with the seven plots nearest to Ham Lane. On one visit we saw a local estate agent taking some people around the site, and as Julie commented in her work later: 'starting with the houses near the road is a very good idea as it is a good advertisement for the builders'.

We had planned to build our own little house in the school grounds to see how it was done. For weeks children lugged bricks to school. Dino brought a brick a day for ten days all the way from home. Fathers, uncles, grandfathers, all found bricks for the children to bring. We had a good collection of assorted colours and ages; the pile was quite impressive. There were too many to house in the classroom so we stored them outside. I was trying to work out how much all the sand and cement would cost to keep these bricks together. The time arrived for the planning of the house. 'But where are the bricks?' asked Dino. Suddenly we were aware that all our precious bricks had disappeared. No-one could tell us where they had gone. Gloom and despondency filled the classroom. The months of transporting all those bricks had been to no avail. Persons unknown must have helped themselves, after school hours – only a broken one remained. It was too late to collect more, so we were denied the pleasure of mixing mortar and laying the bricks for our own house. It was sad for all of us, but the children got over their disappointment soon enough.

As the last Friday of the term approached I was asked: 'It's Friday tomorrow, are we going to the building site?' The pattern had been set and for these children Friday is synonymous with visiting day.

The organisation of work within my class is based upon groups working from assignments. I find that the children like this and that better work develops as a result. This particular study

evolved along such lines with the children working at it whenever they wished. The assignment cards were designed to give
the children ample experience in mathematics, language and
modelling. I found it a most interesting few months. The subject
was far from exhausted but the work we did was often spon-
taneous and usually lively. Working in this fashion meant
preparation. Everything had to be ready to hand and the children
had to know what they were doing. This applied to the teacher
also. When this situation had been established everything ran
comparatively smoothly.

Mathematics

There was plenty of scope for a wide range of mathematics
exercises to be carried out. The length of the lane was estimated,
and then the nursery assistant took Andrew and Sally down the
full length. They counted their paces: 900 in all. Later we
measured an average pace and although the children would not
have arrived at this conclusion on their own, the lane was found
to be about 450 metres in length, probably a little less.

The width of the existing lane was measured and the new road
measured across where it had been completed.

Kerb stones to be laid and paving slabs were all measured.
Bricks were measured and tapes went around the trunks of the
trees.

On the weighing table they had sand and gravel in addition
to their normal things. Bricks of all descriptions were weighed
and they were found to be approximately 3 kilogrammes each.
We had a breeze block to weigh but we did not have the right
apparatus to weigh it.

For 'clock' work we used to time the men unloading various
lorries. Sometimes they had bricks and pipes, sand, gravel and
cement. The gravel lorries were always the quickest and the
brick and pipe lorries the slowest.

The workmen had about an hour for their lunch: 12.30 p.m.–
1.30 p.m., and sometimes 1 p.m.–2 p.m.

For timing, the children used their own watches. Six possessed
these.

As our collection of mini toys grew (things we had seen up

and down the lane) I noticed the children putting them into 'sets':

(a) steamroller, hydraulic roller, wheelbarrow, and crane
(b) handroller, GPO telephone van, theodolite and mechanical digger
(c) cement tanker, gravel lorry, scrapers.

I asked what it was all about. Apparently set (a) were the things we had seen at the road works, set (b) at the building site, and set (c) we had seen in both places.

At this I asked them to draw pictures of all these things and cut them out. Meanwhile I drew two large circles overlapping them. I painted one blue and one yellow. The children were watching at this stage and they saw the common part of both circles change to green. That was a stimulus for something else: for they experimented with mixing colours, and some good brushwork patterns evolved.

When the circles were dry the children played at making up their sets: one colour for the road works, the other for the building site and in the green part they put the things that they had seen in both places.

I watched several groups do this and I was amazed how hard it was for some. After several days of playing at it we stuck them in the appropriate places and put it on the wall. Another copy was put in the Mathematics Book.

We found out a little about how things like sand, gravel, cement, glass and wood are bought. A cubic metre of sand was not easy for them to understand and weights in tonnes were impossible for them to comprehend. They had no practical experience of how heavy a tonne is.

The shop was a marvellous part of the classroom for developing practical experience. The children learnt to handle money and shopping cards well. They were sensible, using real coins, and had far more respect for it than they would have had if they had used cardboard replicas. A few coins were lost but found later.

Some cards told them what to buy. Others left the choice to them. In some cases they had to spend all their money, e.g. 'What can I buy for five new pence?' In others they had to work out the change they required. The largest amount of money they dealt with was twenty-five new pence.

Craft

These children are good at art and craft and throughout the project have done some very good work. It is typically six-year-old infant work — plenty of colour, large and bold. They use block poster colour, pastels, inks and crayons, often all these media on one picture. Inks are the particular favourite at the moment. They use them sensibly; only one spillage has occurred.

In the first term the children made things as they pleased, and the wall pictures were the only things that formed part of the project.

In the second term we started by setting up the shop. Strong plastic bags were filled with sand (ten scoops) and others with gravel (four scoops). Cement was made by mixing grey powder paint with flour. This was cheaper than the real thing and looked most effective. An old demisting panel from the rear window of a car was used for the glass. I cut it with the guillotine as I wanted clean sharp edges and good right angle corners. The wooden planks were cut up by four boys from a length of 3 cm × 2 cm softwood. They measured each piece 3 cm long and then cut it with a hacksaw. This saw they find very easy to use, much better than the strip wood saw.

The putty was made from salt and flour pastry. Flour and salt was mixed with water in a ratio of 1 lb of flour to $\frac{1}{2}$ lb of salt. Then the mixture was baked in a slow oven until very hard. The children did this with no help at all and thoroughly enjoyed themselves.

I had told the children that bricks are made of clay so we used clay for ours. They fashioned the clay into fairly uniform lumps and pressed a piece of wood into the top and bottom to give the authentic look. When they were dry they were painted. We have no kiln so they were left unfired.

When the shop opened the bricks being bought (and dropped) started to break at an alarming rate so we decided to make a second lot out of pastry, otherwise we should have been without bricks by the end of the week.

A small frieze was made entitled 'Shopping in a Builders' Merchants'. It was three-dimensional in effect. In the foreground were heaps of sand and gravel, built up gradually with Evostick as the bonding agent. Bricks were cut from expanded polystyrene ceiling tiles and then painted. They were stuck on with heavy-duty polycel. 'Planks of wood' were strips of balsa wood used for lightness. The people were easy to make. A figure was drawn on card and then cut out. To dress the figure the children selected a piece of material roughly to size for the trousers/shirt/skirt. The part that was to be dressed was glued and then the material stuck on. This continued until the figure was clothed. Then it was left to dry and pressed flat. When it was dry, the child cut round the original shape of the figure, a task needing sharp scissors. Hair might be wool, fur, raffia, feathers or string. Buttons and belts, etc. were added after the figure was cut out.

To give added effect some figures might be placed on distance blocks to bring them out, leaving others in the background. Balsa wood or matchboxes are good distance pieces as they are light and stick easily.

The nursery assistant wanted to have a group of children make a 'junk project' for her NNEB Course. It suited both our purposes that we should do a building site. She bought a piece of hardboard 120 cm × 60 cm and her husband mounted it on a 2 × 2 cm wooden frame, otherwise it would have warped badly. The hardboard was soaked with glue, polycel mixed up by the bucket, and papier mache put on. The children copied the field as well as they could. There was a huge 'dump' at one end and a smaller one at the other. At the beginning no-one particularly wanted to put their hands in the gooey mess, but after a while there were far too many up to their armpits in it.

It was a fortnight later before the model was dry enough to paint.

Trees were made by stripping twigs of their leaves and replacing them with crepe paper leaves. Some had yellow wool catkins on. The trees were then set in place behind the big dump in thickly mixed polyfilla. When dry this was painted brown and the river, running through them, was painted too.

A ceiling tile was cut and stuck down to resemble the foundations of a house. Bricks were cut out from another tile and painted orange. Some were stuck, with heavy-duty polycel, on the foundation to show the walls and the rest were stuck in a large pile beside the workmen's hut, as the children had seen them on the site.

Piles of sand and gravel were made by putting a pile of

polyfilla down and sprinkling the surface whilst still wet with sand or gravel. Polyfilla will stick to other surfaces if you wet them thoroughly first.

The workmen's hut was a small shoe box painted black with a piece of ceiling tile for a roof and a matchbox for a door. The roof was black, until Janelle painted it with multi-coloured blobs of poster paint. Green windows finished the psychedelic effect.

A large tipper lorry and cement tanker were made by Andrew and David. Evostick was the main sticking agent. Dino made the scraper. The children did the work on their own, but the nursery assistant was always to hand as this was her project.

The figures were made out of clay. The use of clay is a craft on its own and I taught the children the way to handle this excellent modelling medium.

It was interesting to see how individual children managed to cope. Michael — a slow learning child — put more thought and concentration into the making of his man than he had ever shown before. He worked for an hour, tongue between his teeth, until he had finished. Julie, on the other hand, a very clever, intelligent girl, was thoroughly frustrated because she could not get the result she wanted. She was positively bad tempered when she finished and walked away not having made anything at all. Dino's foreman was rather like a Colossus.

When the figures were dry the children painted them. Some were very plain; others were resplendent in vibrant colours. Nigel in particular finished his man complete with shovel. Perhaps the flower power clothes of his eldest brother inspired him.

Many children found that standing models were top heavy and they collapsed, so we had a good number sitting down with bowls of soup, cups of tea and one was even reading a newspaper. When all was complete the model was full of life and colour, not in proportion, but with children of this age, things seldom are.

Nature

Old Ham Lane used to be a profitable place for a nature walk, with hedgerows full of interest and the lovely woods at the bottom. The woods are private property and we had to ask for permission to visit there. Now things have changed. As a result of our visits, however, many pictures, stories and descriptions were forthcoming.

Some newts appeared one morning, apparently from the out-of-bounds pond in Ham Woods. I made no comment but accepted them gladly. Towards the end of term we had a very successful trip to the woods. It was a very hot day and the newts were obviously uncomfortable in the classroom. We decided to take them down to the stream, following a route which took us through part of the lane that led to the beach. It was so cool and shady under the trees. The newts were freed, and we rested in the shade, quietly listening to the sounds and observing what movement there was. Some good accounts of this walk were written when we returned. I feel, however, that we did not do as much as we could have done. We could have had a class garden, found specimens in the school grounds, collected leaves and drawn some leaf prints, made bark rubbings, and so on. These things were not neglected on purpose — they just did not happen. We were always busy at something else and, had there been a dull period, no doubt I would have introduced some of the above activities.

It is through a rich, colourful and interesting classroom that many children when they commence school are first introduced to their surroundings. They should be able to learn in a workshop situation and be given the opportunity to explore, communicate and record their experiences. By the time they have reached the upper classes of the infant school their interests should have widened to make possible some simple investigation of the locality in which they live and some appreciation of the simple phenomena of the world around them. This process will permit the children to practise and extend the basic skills they will have already gained.

This is the broad philosophy that I apply to the study of the environment by the two hundred pupils of the infants' school in which I work. The village in which the school is situated lies along the boundary of two counties and originated during the industrial expansion of the early 19th century. On the southern perimeter of the village a modern highway has diverted the heavy flow of traffic that once clogged the narrow streets. To the north and west there is a coalmine, and a large site for factories producing an assortment of goods. Limestone quarries abound, a few of which are still being worked. Mountains are a feature that can be seen, but open-cast mining has destroyed even this beauty in parts. Most of the houses are stone built and date back to the origin of the village with no thought of planning. With redevelopment many lie empty waiting for demolition, while their occupants have been transferred to a modern housing estate on the outskirts of the village.

Five years ago, in spite of ample land being available, tower block flats were built. Naturally, the majority of the occupants of these are married couples with young children. They are faced with the problem of not having anywhere for the children to play together. This 20th-century phenomenon is one for which we in the school have to find some compensation. The present state of the local river and its surroundings help us in this respect, for although the water is not crystal clear sufficient life exists in it to make it interesting. Along its banks the foundations of iron workers' cottages have become overgrown with long grass and the remains of once busy furnaces a few yards away can provide us with stories of our village long ago and the children who once attended our school.

The school building is one hundred and twenty-five years old and strenuous efforts have been made to improve its quality, but of course we are left with such problems as being unable to gaze through the windows because of the height from the floor and the warren-like nature of the building. Consequently, the colourful and interesting classroom that I mentioned at the outset is very necessary as one of the compensatory features that must be provided.

Before the study of the river was made by this class of 6–7-year-olds a large model of the district had been made. This was on a hardboard base two metres long and one metre wide. We had laid down small mesh wire in roughly the shape of the land. Over this had been pasted successive layers of paper allowing each layer to dry before applying the next. Roads, river and other prominent features were then painted on and buildings were represented by matchbox houses. The river had been a prominent feature of the model. Alongside the model was a large number of work cards devised and produced by the teacher so that the children could use it in a practical manner. These work cards gave them experience in relating the positions of buildings to their school and home, practice in reading, measuring and writing simple descriptions.

On a sheet of paper the same size as the model, that is two metres by one metre, the children and I made a map of the village showing many of the features seen on the model, including the river which runs through the centre. Inevitably, the children wanted their houses marked on the map and so, after discussion with the class teacher, they decided to represent them with red squares, the village schools in brown, the farms in green, church with a cross, and so on. They enjoyed locating their streets and houses and using the work cards in the same manner as on the model. (The map was subsequently pinned to the wall behind the model.) David, who crossed from one county to the other on his way to school, decided to find how many different routes he could take. He used the map to show the rest of the children his routes.

The river was a few minutes walk from the school and so we decided to pay it a visit. As headteacher I feel it is my duty to accompany teachers on all expeditions with children of this age. The section of the river to which we went is ideal for children.

There is a large bend with a pebble stretch, a section of stagnant water and some swift flowing water (low enough in summer to be perfectly safe). On either side there are fields with animals, old ironwork kilns, countless trees and bushes and over the river a footbridge — an ideal situation indeed. We wandered around frequently discussing all the things to be observed and although the area was familiar to most of the children we were presented with many questions. How deep is the river? How wide is it? Whose field is that? Can we throw stones in the river? Where does it go? The chatter of children disturbed the peace of the lazy summer afternoon and it gave a few of the more robust boys a grand opportunity to hold an impromptu wrestling match in the grass. At the end of it all, however, we had collected some pebbles, flowers, leaves and a number of caterpillars.

On our return to school we talked again about some of the things we had seen and the children gathered into one pile the simple reference books that could give us some of the answers to their questions. Questions such as 'Where does all the water come from?' led to a simple explanation of how rain is formed. A special display of relevant reference books was made and the children formed into groups based upon their interests and varying ability.

The river group   To make a model of the river and the surrounding features (fig. 3)

The collage group   To make a collage picture showing how rivers are made (from melting snow, ice, rain, springs, etc)

The stones group   To collect and grade stones found on the pebbly bank of the river according to size, colour, shape, texture (fig. 4)

The flower and tree group   To collect flowers and leaves of trees that grow near the river, to press and label them, and to make lists of flowers found each week

The second river group   To make a model of a section of the river and the creatures and plant life common to it

All models are constructed mainly of junk, reinforced in some instances by the real thing. For example, the second river group placed real pebbles at the bottom of their model. Children who were slow in discussion and written work were encouraged to assist in the construction of the models but every opportunity was taken to involve simple vocabulary exercises based upon their activities. Certainly there was the usual increase in communication between teacher and pupils in this situation.

During one of the frequent periods of conversation dealing with the study we were making, Richard asked, 'Where does the river come from?' Jane then followed this by asking, 'Where does it go?' To illustrate the answers the teacher made a rough sketch showing the river passing through towns and villages to the sea. Many of the children had relations living in some of these so we were told orally and in writing about these people. We went to a vantage point close by to look at the river winding from the source in one direction and towards the sea in the other. The children shaded in the map with crayons; all place names were printed on pieces of paper which were in turn pasted on to the map. Later on the map was reproduced by using pieces of felt to represent the river, hills, etc, and the names were again printed on thin card backed by felt. This became our flannelgraph map of the course of the river. Words such as source, course and estuary were introduced and placed upon the map.

The different activities involved many visits to the river by small groups of children. Little difficulty is experienced as far as this is concerned as long as all are prepared to co-operate and the pupils are used to working without continuous direction. The group books included such titles as:

How we made our model
How rivers are made
Creatures of a river
Our visits to the river
Our stories about a river
River stories we enjoyed.

A large vocabulary of new words was acquired. The children were able, on their various visits, to observe the water cascading, shimmering, rippling, gurgling, babbling, leaping, glistening, sparkling. They understood these words from personal experience. Our *River News*, a supplement to the school newspaper, described visits to the river, the making of a model, and so on.

Work cards were prepared for use by groups and individuals. Here are samples of the assignments:

(1) Describe one of your visits to the river
(2) Tell me one of the ways in which a river is made
(3) Make a list of words to describe the stones we have collected
(4) How many words can you think of to describe a river?

Games based upon the ability of the children to relate pictures to words and words to words were used, many of these devised by the staff and used extensively by the slower pupils. One game consisted of a square board of thirty-six squares, each square comprising a picture of an animal or plant found near the river. Thirty-six cards containing the name only were then placed on the appropriate squares. Sometimes this activity would be given to an individual and at other times to two, three or four players, the aim being to see who finished first. Another game consisted of a similar board on which were pasted pictures of the homes of creatures found near the river. Two sets of cards were made for this, one containing the name of the home and the other the name of the creature. This game could provide a number of variations for the individual child or a group of children.

We always make apparatus such as this from thick card and use sheets of clear gum-backed plastic to protect it from the extensive handling it gets.

A great deal of mathematical activity stemmed from the study. All the children were given the opportunity of sorting the stones they had collected; big — little; rough — smooth; hard — soft; rounded — irregular; brown — grey. Mathematics work cards, using metric measure, were compiled to give the children opportunities of using acquired skills in new situations. These cards involved making number relationships, weighing, measuring length, width, perimeter and area.

(1) How long is the river in the model?
(2) Measure its width at the narrowest and widest parts
(3) How high is the bridge over the river?
(4) What is the perimeter of Bainton's field?
(5) How many shapes can you see in the model? Make a graph to show how many of each shape you have found

Much of this work was repeated in a real situation and groups were able to measure the depth of the river under the bridge, the height of the bridge, the width of the river at selected points and so on. They found out how quickly the river flowed where it was swift flowing and where it was calmer. They compared the time taken by floating a paper boat over a measured distance. These results were recorded in our book *How we measured the river*.

Picture books were made showing examples of rivers in all parts of the world and these were frequently used as interesting discussion points. Inevitably we talked about the different uses made of rivers, which led to the use of 'our river' and the making of iron a hundred years ago. We walked along the old tram lines that had carried coal and iron ore; we collected pieces of smooth coloured slag and we were able to look at old prints of the works. This, however, is another story.

With a little forethought children of all abilities were able to participate in and enjoy the study, strengthening and developing their knowledge and understanding of their locality while at the same time improving their skills in reading, writing and mathematics.

The Background to the Study

The children with whom I carried out this work were a mixed ability group of thirty pupils, aged 9 to 11 years. They comprised the top class of a Junior and Infant School of one hundred and twenty pupils of which I was the teaching head. The remainder of the pupils were divided into three classes, each with its assistant teacher. The building was erected in the 1880's to serve the children of the families who settled in the area as a result of the then flourishing coal mining industry. The classrooms were all extremely small and cramped but some of the children could use the hall when the time-table permitted.

I devoted two afternoons per week to environmental studies and this formed the basis of most of the work in the traditional curriculum areas of history, geography, science and nature study. A careful, scientific examination of the locality was used as a base for wider concentric studies using the skills developed. In addition, however, a great deal of work in English, mathematics, art, etc, arose from the work produced.

I had long since built up a reference library at the school and also had acquired local area maps of various scales, together with items of equipment necessary in an approach of this nature. The children who carried out this study were well acquainted with many of the skills required from experience in lower classes.

Preparation and initial class expedition

My idea in choosing a belt transect was that it could serve two purposes. First of all it was an obvious development from the previous year's work and secondly it could act as a regional summary.

I duplicated simplified 25-inch-to-the-mile maps of the area to be studied. These showed cardinal points, field boundaries, roads, buildings, footpaths and, in particular, the route we should follow during our initial walk. As a class we studied these maps and I pointed out some of the landmarks we should be seeing, with a few words of explanation.

During the walk I took the opportunity of drawing the children's attention to:

(a) Orientation of maps, so that the children could relate what

was shown on their maps to the countryside around them
(b) The relation of symbols on the map to specific objects on
the ground
(c) The meanings of such words and phrases as undulating
land, steep sided valley, etc, by pointing out actual
examples as we came across them
(d) The direction in which we were walking. This they could
discover from their maps
(e) Estimated distances, which we checked by measuring on
the ground' and on the maps (exercise in using scale).

One of the first things we observed on the walk was evidence
of old industrial activity in the form of an old colliery bank, a
cutting of an old tramway, and the site of an old smelt works
which operated in the late 18th and early 19th centuries. We
saw the local coal department, with its stocks of different types
of coal, and shortly afterwards passed a line of low mounds in
the field. These were old disused air shafts, and this suggested
to us that we were following the line of the old underground
level that ran from a nearby village to the colliery which was
situated immediately behind the school. (I knew this level
existed.) We observed and noted the crops, animals and any
farming activity in the fields.

Before us lay the valley of the local river, and I was able to
point out to the children some of the features mentioned in (c)
above. We continued our walk down the side of the valley,
crossing the disused railway line – further evidence of industrial
activity in the area. Later we studied old maps of the area, but we
had already noticed from the 25-inch map that there had been
an extensive and complex system of railways and tramways
serving local industry – none of which now exists. In our later
study of the old maps of the area we discovered that there had
been a great number of mines and other works in existence, all
of which, except one, had now closed.

Down in the neighbouring village, we noticed how the new
council houses had been built in keeping with the rest of the
village, which consisted mainly of old houses. The council
houses were very different in style from the ones built in our
village. The children noticed this and the question was posed,
'Why was this?' We observed briefly the amount of traffic on the

main roads, and compared them with the quieter roads of our area.
Finally we reached the river near its confluence with a smaller stream. Nearby was a sewage works and two bridging points over the river, one being the present road bridge and the other the older bridge and route which it replaced. We followed this old road for a little distance in order to see the ruins of an old corn mill to which the farmers on the local estate had brought their corn for grinding. We had unexpected help from an old gentleman who showed us the mill race and spoke to the children about the mill, and from the licensee of the *Bridge Inn*, who showed us where the horses used to be watered and stabled, and told us something of its history as a coaching inn.

Follow-up Work
In the classroom we discussed some of the things we had observed on the walk. For instance, a comparison was made between the 'industrial village' (i.e. a village that had grown as a result of local industry) and the older village near the crossroads and bridge that came within our belt transect, with its rural background, its tied cottages and close connections with the large estate of the local landowner.

Other aspects of the exercise were discussed and other comparisons made before the class proceeded to draw a transect of the selected area. The children, who had previous experience of making a transect, were divided into groups, and worked at the following tasks:

(a) A cross-section or profile of the area, which measured four hundred metres in width and one-and-a-half kilometres in length
(b) A physical map of the area. Heights to be indicated by means of contour lines and colours
(c) A map showing land use, i.e. agricultural, waste, woodland and built-up land
(d) A map showing types of farming carried on in the area
(e) A map showing communications. Main roads, second-class roads and footpaths.

The scale chosen was: horizontal 20 cm represented 1 km; vertical 1 cm represented 20 m.

This exercise did not take long to complete, and the children then decided what aspect of the topic they would like to pursue further. The groups were formed according to their interests, and decided they would like to study the following topics:

The local river
Roads and transport
The old colliery bank
Farming
The village.

Group I   The Local River
The group visited the river at a suitable stretch and embarked upon such tasks as measuring the width of the river (this was done at a bridging point, and further down the river with an angle meter), measuring the depth of the river at four different points across the river· (again at a bridging point with a weighted line), measuring the speed of the river in miles per hour by timing a floating object, measuring the length of the section of river we were studying, noting and marking on a sketch map the type of vegetation in the vicinity of the river (mainly types of trees and grasses). The children performed these tasks singly, in pairs or sometimes as a group.

I was able here to illustrate the meanings of such words as meandering, eroding, deposition, since the river very obligingly did all these things on the section we were studying.

Follow-up Work   The group again split up and worked singly or in pairs, explaining and illustrating how they had accomplished their various tasks on the visit to the river. The work produced included:

(a) An illustrated account of how the depth of the river was found
(b) A section drawn across the river bed (from measurements of the depth of the river)
(c) A scale plan of this section of the river showing currents, rapids, slower stretches, deposition of stones and gravel, and surrounding vegetation
(d) An illustrated account of how the speed of the river was found. The children came to an approximate answer at

the river, but the exact speed was worked out in class, and also the time it would take the water to reach the River Dee and eventually the sea at this speed.

Development of Work   The children in the group were then allowed to choose for themselves the direction in which they wished their work to develop. They are at present involved in the completion of this study, and I list below some of the work being carried out:

    (a) A study of settlements and industries on the banks of the river

    (b) How water is brought to our homes. A study of reservoirs and water supplies

    (c) Fresh water fish – starting with the fish to be found in the local river

    (d) A study of trees and natural vegetation to be found in the vicinity of the river

    (e) A study of other rivers in Wales, Britain and the world.

Group II   Roads and Transport
This group began by carrying out a traffic count on the main road, noting the number of vehicles of different types, the registration numbers of the vehicles, and the places of origin of the lorries and vans from the names written on the sides.

Follow-up Work   The children in this group again worked individually or in pairs. Examples of some of the work carried out included:

    (a) A graph showing the numbers of different types of vehicles

    (b) A graph showing the places of origin of the vehicles. The information was obtained by looking up the registration numbers in an AA book

    (c) A map showing the places of origin of vehicles, and the number of vehicles from different areas of the British Isles by means of small red squares. One square represented one vehicle.

This exercise was repeated on another main road, and a

comparison made of the numbers of various types of vehicles using these two main roads, one of which runs approximately North/South parallel to the border, and the other NE–SW. The places of origin of the vehicles were also studied. This comparative study proved very interesting because of the marked differences which were evident from a study of the graphs and maps, both in the types of vehicles and their places of origin.

Group III   The Old Colliery behind the School

This group decided to begin by having a look at the old colliery bank behind the school, and at the same time to find out as much as they could about the history of the colliery from the old people of the village, some of whom had worked there. I went in search of information to the County Records Office but found out very little indeed. The children found out a great deal more about this, and about other old works in the district, and began writing historical accounts of the colliery from the information they had gathered.

In the meantime they had begun looking at the bank itself, and the first thing they wanted to do was to find its height. They made a simple angle meter. Then they measured the angle from the school yard to the top of the bank, and the distance along the ground between these two points (along a lane which runs beside the school and the bank). By means of a scale drawing they calculated the height of the bank.

They decided they would also like to measure and record the other 'vital statistics' of the bank, so they measured its length and width and calculated its area. They also wished to calculate the approximate amount of material contained in the bank, but owing to its irregular shape this posed some difficulty, and has not yet been achieved!

From an old map of the area, dated 1871, the children were able to see how the coal was transported from the colliery by means of a tramway to the main railway line. A cutting along which the tramway ran is still in existence near the school, and its presence there had previously puzzled the children. An account of how the empty trucks were pulled up the gradient back to the colliery by the weight of the loaded trucks going down the gradient to the main railway line had been obtained previously by the children when they were gathering information about the colliery. One of the boys brought a model railway to school, and the children were able to observe for themselves how this system worked. A map was then drawn of the area showing the extensive railway system, the tramways leading from the collieries to the main railway, and the location of industries in and around the village.

This group then decided they would like to find out something about coal mining today. They sent for some pamphlets from the NCB, and researched into coal mining in their reference books. They produced illustrated accounts as a result of their studies, and drew a map showing the mines still working, and the mines recently closed on the North Wales Coalfield.

They were also interested in the distribution of coal, so I arranged a visit to the local coalman, who has a coal storage depot behind his home. The children had previously observed the coal depot filled with different types of coal on their initial walk. They had noticed that the depot was full in the summer, but, for reasons economic and climatic, much less so in the winter. The children had previously prepared the questions they wished to ask, but they were not able to get answers to all their questions. For instance we were not able to find out how much coal was delivered to the depot each week or month, or to find out on average how much was sold. However, quite a lot of interesting information was obtained on where the coalman got his coal, the types of coal, the names of the various sizes of coal, how it was delivered to him, where he delivered the coal, etc, and a fair amount of follow-up work resulted from this visit. More work could have been done, of course, had we known the actual amounts of coal involved. Two maps were produced showing:

(a) The collieries supplying coal to our coalman; these were in the North Wales and Staffordshire coalfields

(b) Where our coalman delivers coal (i.e. specific villages and areas).

Development of the Work   A study of the following topics, beginning with the local area where applicable, and developing to include the North Wales coalfield and then the whole of

Britain. Some aspects, of course, can be extended to give a world-wide picture.

(a) The story of coalmining. Historical approach
(b) Coal mining today. Modern methods of mining, etc
(c) Uses of coal. Past and present
(d) Reasons for decline of the coal industry
(e) Other forms of power that have replaced coal

Group IV   Farming
This group decided to find out what kind of farming was being practised in our selected area. They already had the outline maps that I had duplicated for the initial exercise. We discussed in class what we were going to look for in the fields, and decided to observe and mark on the maps what was growing in the fields, what animals were in the fields, and what activities were being carried out by the farmer. The children would also mark on their maps whether there were hedges or fences, areas of woodland, waste land, and gardens. A way of recording the information while out in the fields was agreed upon, and this was a simple use of letters − G = grass, A = arable, etc, with a note on type of crop, and types of animals, if any.

Follow-up Work   A key was decided upon, this time using colours instead of letters, e.g. Grass − green, Arable − brown, Woodland − dark green, Gardens − purple, Wasteland − yellow, etc, and letters were used for the types of animals found in the fields in this way: D − Dairy Cattle, S − Stock Cattle, SH − Sheep. The children were given fresh outline maps, and using the notes they had made on the exercise, coloured their maps in. Written accounts were made of the work done so far, and a certain amount of analysis carried out on the type of farming practised in the selected area. Diagrams and graphs were drawn showing use of land, and types and numbers of animals observed in the fields.

A visit to a local farm with fields in our selected area
Each member of the group read and prepared questions about different aspects of farming. I had visited the farm the previous year, and had a good idea of what they would find there.

Questions were prepared about (a) Sheep, (b) Cattle, (c) Pigs, (d) Poultry, (e) Crops grown, (f) Rotation of Crops, (g) Marketing and buying of stock and produce, etc.
During the visit the farmer was really most co-operative. He showed the children everything there was to show, explained everything in detail and answered all questions. The children took notes and made sketches.

Follow-up Work
(a) Written accounts of the visit
(b) A map of the farm and fields, showing what crops were growing in the fields
(c) Diagrams and graphs showing the use of the land, and the number of animals kept on the farm
(d) A map showing the rotation of crops
(e) Written accounts and diagrams of the type of farming carried on at this farm

Development of Work   This group has not reached the stage of developing the work further. There are many ways, of course, in which it could develop, I shall outline but two:
(a) A further study of farming in Britain by taking sample studies of farms in other parts of the country – a sample study involving a farm representative of its area and of a type of farming. I have in school sample studies of:

(i) An upland farm on the Welsh Border
(ii) A dairy farm in Somerset
(iii) An arable farm in Norfolk.

Comparisons can be made with one's own area. The topic can be enlarged still further to include:

(i) Rice growing in Japan
(ii) Cattle breeding on the Argentine Pampas
(iii) Wheat growing on the Canadian Prairies, etc, etc, thus giving the children a wider understanding of agriculture.

(b) The second way in which the work could develop is by the children, either singly, in pairs or as a group, pursuing one particular produce, e.g. wheat again, and finding out all they could about how this commodity is grown and marketed throughout the world.

Group V   Our Village

Preparation

(a) I duplicated large scale, freehand maps of the part of the village that we were going to study, and considered them in detail with the children.

(b) We discussed what we were going to observe and record and decided upon:
  (i) Types of buildings — whether houses, shops, chapels, garages, post office or public houses
  (ii) Age of buildings — old or new. This can prove difficult if a suitable area is not chosen
  (iii) Building materials — whether bricks, stone, wood, concrete — and roofing materials — slate, tiles, etc.

(c) We decided on symbols to record information.

Exercise   This consisted of the children observing and recording information according to the tasks allocated to them. The children worked in pairs; I again took the opportunity of doing a little practical map work as on previous outings, e.g. orientation, direction, relation of symbols to objects, finding bench marks, etc.

Follow-up Work   From the information they had recorded, the children drew maps, using colours and symbols showing types of buildings, age of buildings, and building and roofing materials. Written work, graph work on types of buildings and materials, and some analysis followed the making of the maps. For instance the children realised from the information gathered that, although there was ample evidence of past industry in the district, it was no longer an industrial area. People who lived in the village travelled elsewhere to work, and this led to further study.

Examples of further study:
(1) A map showing the position of the village in relation to nearby towns and villages
(2) A map showing the position of the village in relation to the principal towns and cities in the British Isles. The

children chose the cities, asked me if they were suitable, then found the position of these cities from atlases, and marked them on a large outline map of the British Isles, previously marked with concentric circles showing distances from the area

(3) A graph showing the occupations of parents was made, and a map drawn showing where they worked, and how many worked at each place, with circles showing distances from the village. This study arose from the fact that there are no industries in the village

(4) A graph showing how parents travel to work.

(5) A map and graph showing where the children lived in the village. This gave an indication of where young couples with families lived and its relation to the newer property in the village. It showed the distribution and numbers involved

(6) A graph showing how many people to a family, and how many to a house. This showed us where there was overcrowding in the village

(7) Then it was decided to carry the work on the age of buildings further. The whole class gathered information for this group from relatives and friends. The information was checked and further information discovered from some old maps I had been very fortunate to have given to me.

From a map dated 1899 the children were able to see which were the 19th century buildings, and from a 1918 map they could see which were the pre-First World War houses. The buildings were grouped in the following manner: pre-1900, 1900–1914, 1918–1939, and post-war buildings. They were recorded on a map in different colours, showing an interesting pattern of development in the village. A graph was drawn to represent this information, and this showed a steady increase in building over the years, and especially since the Second World War. This particular study led to class lessons on the Industrial Revolution, the British Empire in the 19th century, and social, housing and working conditions of the time.

Development of Work

(a) The children will try to find out where the bricks that were used to build the houses came from, and this will lead to a study of the brick-making industry

(b) Similar studies involving the slate and timber industries

Final Comment

The work that I have referred to in these notes has been done mainly in the time allocated to environmental studies on the timetable. I have intentionally omitted any reference to work done in English, art, mathematics and nature study arising from environmental studies, but this type of work does have a great stimulating effect on many subjects in the school curriculum. The outings I have mentioned led to countless opportunities for descriptive writing and creative writing in English as well as factual accounts; they led to calculation, graph work and dia-grammatic representation in mathematics; they led to oppor-tunities for painting in the art lessons, model making in the craft lessons and studies of natural vegetation, river life, etc, in nature study. The oral reports and the careful display of work that followed the completion of each investigation were also found to be of great value to the children.

The hamlet in which I was teaching when this study was carried out is situated in a remote part of Wales. Consisting of a handful of houses and a small chapel, it is out of sight of the school and approximately two hundred yards away. A slightly larger village is situated a mile and a half away and is the centre for the social life of the area. The rolling hills, river valley and pockets of woodland all contribute to the panoramic beauty of the neighbourhood. Activities readily available to colleagues in urban areas are denied to us. We rarely see any traffic except the occasional farm tractor or herd of cows, and visitors are rare and welcome. Many compensatory features, however, exist for both children and adults.

The school itself had fifty-three children on roll when this study took place. There were twenty-eight between the ages of 5 and 7 years and twenty-five between the ages of 7 and 11 years. As full-time teaching head I was responsible for the top group; a second teacher was responsible for the infants and a third teacher attended for five mornings per week, when the younger children were divided into two groups. The original building was erected nearly one hundred years ago and consisted of one large room. A few years ago a modernization scheme was completed so that the large room was split into two by the addition of a soundproof partition, and a new classroom, toilets and entrance foyer were added. The junior department was housed in this new room which is pleasant, has large windows and is well ventilated.

The majority of the pupils travel considerable distances to attend school, some as much as six miles. Occasionally the school is used by local organisations but this does not interfere with the day-to-day running of the school. The school's pride and joy is, without doubt, the swimming pool which is sited on the edge of the play area and is bordered on three sides by grass. Complete with filtration plant it has always proved a boon to the pupils of the area.

Throughout almost the whole of my professional career I had attempted to use the locality in which I worked. I have always felt that children should, under the guidance of the teacher, study their neighbourhood to investigate local phenomena and extend their studies further afield. This is very important for children living in isolated parts of the country. We had previously investigated the history of the school, and its position in relation to the village, the farms and further afield the distant towns. To do all this we had used the school log book and found how people had lived over a period of one hundred years. We had examined old plans of the school, the materials that had gone into the construction of the school, both old and new. The water, gas and electricity supplies had been studied. Road maps and county maps had been used to find the distances of farms, villages and towns from the school, which had developed work on scale and graphs. We had also constructed a simple bearing table and, as the school is sited in an elevated position, it gave the younger children an opportunity to use the table on copses, farms and mountains.

Most of the time the children worked in four groups of mixed ages and abilities with one responsible pupil in charge of each. I hovered in the background suggesting, guiding, asking pertinent questions and frequently helping the younger pupils.

I wanted the children to make a study of the hamlet and, with the experience they already had, we were able to wander along the hundred yard main street. One child noticed that, although the village is on a hill, it lacks a sign showing the gradient. This later gave rise to a step-survey of the hill using two jumping canes graduated in feet. During our walk we took the opportunity of chatting to the locals, who were curious to know what we were doing. As usual, full co-operation was forthcoming. From previous experience, the younger children knew that they were to obtain permission before posing questions to people.

It was decided to investigate four main aspects of the village: the hill, the buildings, the inhabitants and, lastly, the bridge over the river. This meant that four groups could operate again and that each group would be of mixed ability and age. I spoke to each group in turn and discussed some of the lines they might follow, while the other three groups sat and listened. Occasionally a member of another group would offer a comment and some wanted to change groups, particularly when they realised that a small number were going to spend some time by the river (apart from other delights it was full of trout). At this stage, however, I needed to be firm so that the study would commence in a reasonably controlled manner. It would be soon enough to allow greater flexibility once the work was progressing smoothly. This was the pattern I had adopted on previous occasions and I saw no reason to alter it at this time.

We descended on the area a few days later armed with note books, home-made clinometers, tapes, a measuring chain and the usual paraphernalia necessary on a visit of this sort. The group dealing with the hill immediately broke up into two distinct groups. The older children began to step survey the hill while the younger ones began to collect specimen flowers and plants from the hedgerow at the side. They were soon attracted to the older pupils when they saw what an apparently important job they were doing. I helped stimulate this interest by giving one of the canes to a seven-year-old to hold. A plan of the street was drawn eventually and all the buildings marked. We varied this map by reproducing it to show the age of the buildings, their materials and purpose they served. Old Ordnance Survey maps and even the Tithe map were useful in this respect. This stretch of road was formerly part of an old drovers' route and this led to a great deal of very interesting work on the 18th- and 19th-century cattle trade between England and Wales. One of the houses had been *The Drovers' Arms* many years ago and another still exists not too far away.

Little could be carried out in the hamlet in the way of a census of traffic because of its scarcity but a group of children living near a main road carried out a census over a weekend so that at least comparisons could take place and reasons for the differences be discussed.

The group studying the inhabitants made a census and then analysed this according to occupations, sex, names, religion, etc, and recorded the data in a variety of ways. Simple maps showing where people worked were drawn and we talked about the non-existence of public transport. One man had recently become the owner of a vintage car which he was renovating and this led to a study of forms of transport that the village had seen. The use of the area for low flying exercises gave the pupils an opportunity to compare the ancient and modern.

By the river, plants, stones, insects and all the items that appealed to the children's collecting instincts were brought back to school, mounted or allocated a place in a jar and suitably labelled. The same group found out when the bridge was built, which led them to the origin of the village, namely a site at which the drovers forded the river. This was a point at which I felt rather pleased, for the drovers provided a link between the findings of the 'river' group and the 'hill' group which was quite obvious to the children. In other words they began to realise the unified development of the hamlet; the bridge, the school, the chapel and most of the houses all were built at about the same time.

What of the materials used in the construction of the buildings? We were all aware of the old quarry outside the village, near an old flour mill with its water channel for powering the wheel and the old church which stood near by. The machinery of the mill could still be seen so we were able to follow the grinding of flour through its stages. From the quarry we obtained more specimens of plants and flowers and we were also fortunate in finding some fossils. We took some rubbings of the plaques in the church, one of which recorded the life and death of one Hugonus Morgan, a relation of Henry Morgan the buccaneer. What a find that was, particularly for children so far removed from the sea!

We ventured out into the village whenever we felt we required more information. I was fortunate in that I could frequently allow a small group to leave school when the reason was genuine but only the older pupils were allowed this privilege. Between the school and the top of the hill there was a lane which was 147 metres long. (It had been measured by click wheel, tape, a child's pace and all other known methods, so I can vouch for the accuracy of the figure.) At the end of the lane there was a Victorian post box set in a pillar; the lane and the fields on either side were rich in flora and fauna. I could see the whole of this area from the classroom window and consequently the younger pupils could collect specimens from here without becoming involved in dangerous situations.

As the weeks went by so our store of information grew and was recorded in a variety of media; graphs, wall posters, group books, individual folders, displayed collections of plants and stones, stories from old inhabitants on tape and in written form and models of bridges. Aspects far too numerous to mention here were followed up, sometimes suggested by the children, sometimes by one child only, and occasionally as a result of a comment from one of the inhabitants.

With the wide age range of pupils that I had to cope with,

problems inevitably arose from time to time. These were largely confined to the younger pupils and in the main consisted of their attempts to imitate the older pupils and loss of interest when they failed. Consequently I had to be on the alert all the time, helping, encouraging and praising their efforts. For example, I had to make it obvious to them that although I expected a certain standard of work their finished product would not always be as polished as that of the older children. On other occasions such as model making younger and older pupils worked harmoniously at their different projects. I often spent short periods with the younger pupils showing them different ways of working, while the others carried on with their investigations. The teacher of a class with such a wide age-span has to allow for differences arising from this, and accept work differing according to age. In this he is often helped by the older pupils who generally accept the comparatively limited results of their juniors.

As a way of working, teachers in small schools will agree that there is nothing new in organising a class on this basis. It is exhausting yet often stimulating, frequently interesting and rewarding, and never allowing stagnation.

My school is a large mixed primary of more than 400 pupils, located in a market town in one of the Marcher counties. Studies involving direct use of the environment are undertaken at all levels within the school, using the urban and rural opportunities available.

On a number of occasions I had suggested to groups of children that we might investigate the site of a local Iron Age encampment which can be seen from the playground. The numerous pools near this historical feature had always been used for pond dipping expeditions and perhaps for this reason my suggestions were never accepted with any degree of enthusiasm – a case of familiarity breeding contempt. It was a happy co-incidence for me that immediately before a school term an article appeared in the local press entitled 'Cave gives up its secrets'.

The article dealt with the details of the find of the local antiquarian society as a result of excavations made in a cave located on a hill some ten kilometres away. Among the items discovered were human bones, coins and pottery dating from the Roman occupation, an Edward III silver coin and pieces of 18th-century clay pipes. It was claimed that the Romans had been involved in copper mining in the area. Many of the children were already aware of the contents of the article when I read it to the class shortly after the term began. I think they responded favourably for two reasons: first a visit would entail a journey on a private 'bus and secondly they had visions of a local El Dorado. They were ready to leave then and there but I had other ideas, not the least of which was the necessary preparatory work needed before embarking on a visit to this type of site. There was a 'bus to be ordered, permission to be obtained, and above all I did not want three dozen pupils descending like locusts on such a location and having to put up with the inevitable repercussions. I thought, too, that keeping the class in suspense for a short while would tend to increase their enthusiasm.

I obtained copies of the 25-inch and 6-inch maps of the area so that we could carry out some easy exercise such as making simple route maps. One of these dealt with the 'bus journey from the school to the disembarkation point and the other with the walk from the 'bus to the cave. The class knew how to read a 25-inch map but were not too familiar with the use of the 6-inch.

We examined the position of the hill and inevitably the question of contour lines came up. I had never attempted work on these before and thought that this was as good a time as any to see if the class might understand them. We used potatoes. The children brought one between two and cut it in half. Each child marked off his half in two-centimetre pieces and then sliced off each layer. The outlines of these layers were used to represent contour lines.

(Later on one group of children made a large model of the hill on which the cave was located and this in turn led to some simple work on cross sections.)

While the work on contour lines was going on our enquiries revealed that the land was owned by a limestone quarrying company who in turn had leased it to a golf club. Letters were written to both organisations for permission to cross over their land and this was readily given within two days. A letter was then sent to a local transport firm arranging the booking of a 'bus.

We now returned to the 25-inch map to see if we might locate the easiest route to the cave and also to see what other features could be examined while we were there. As a result of discussion five working parties were formed to investigate the following features:

(1) The cave
(2) Spoil heaps
(3) Plant life
(4) Offa's Dyke
(5) Orientation (relation of cave's position to the general area).

This general planning I had operated before and the class was aware that within reason there would be a considerable degree of flexibility of groups on site. For example, I had to assure them that all would have an opportunity of going in the cave. Three final tasks remained. First, the assembling of the equipment for an expedition such as this; secondly, the distribution of the work cards that had been prepared; and, lastly, warning the class of the dangers, e.g. old lead shafts. Here are some of the pieces of equipment we carried: plastic container for soil samples and plant specimens, anglemeter, hammer, plastic bags, trowel, torches, pocket lenses, binoculars, maps, penknives, wax for rubbings, camera, individual note books and pencils, clay boards with sheets of paper attached by clips for sketching, quadrat frames, surveyor's chain.

For once the chosen day was bright and dry. The 'bus deposited us within a twelve minute walk of the cave and off we went, noticing the features that until now had been lines or dots on a map. Arriving at the spot the groups went quietly to their different locations (fig. 5), with the exception of the children who were allocated the task of examining the cave. They rushed into the cave, while their friends in other groups cast envious glances over their shoulders.

The cave echoed with the excited shrieks of the pupils and all instructions were forgotten. I let them get rid of their nervous excitement and then brought them out again. I reminded them of the tasks it had been decided they would undertake and before long they were carrying these out. Samples of rock and soil were collected, sketches prepared and other tasks referred to on the work cards.

The group examining the spoil heaps went about their tasks much more calmly. Samples of rock containing ores were gathered: plants, insects and anything interesting placed in their containers. I was pleased to see that some of the points I had tried to instill in them on previous occasions were being observed, namely, they were being selective and also limiting their specimens to one example of each. The highlight of the morning for this group was the discovery of what they thought to be the entrance of a fox's earth. Closer examination, resulting in the discovery of traces of hair and footprints, proved beyond all doubt that it was a badger's sett.

Unfortunately, we had not brought any plaster so could not take a cast but a visit later in the week undertaken only by a smaller group resulted in a great deal of work developing in relation to animal tracks.

The children gathering information on plant life were busily using the quadrat frames and taking samples one metre square from the whole area; they gathered specimens and made rough notes on each section. Two pupils using large plastic containers made miniature gardens of each section examined. Later many of their specimens were transplanted in the wild flower garden that had been made in school.

A short distance from the cave the remains of Offa's Dyke

could be seen. I had provided the group who were to examine the ditch and bank with some suggestions and also ensured that they could be relied upon not to come to any harm. They were all able to use apparatus such as the clinometer and surveyor's chain, having been instructed many months prior to this study and having used it on other visits. Again this group made rough notes for follow-up work in class. Their highlight was finding a golf ball on the way back to join the main party.

The hill on which the cave is located is 250 metres above sea level. To the west the mountains of Wales rose towards the sky, while eastwards stretched the plain with its rich agricultural land. The river Severn, a main road running north to south, canal, villages and numerous other features allowing exercises in orientation could be observed from this vantage point. One group made a rough sketch of the site, showing the approximate locations of the badger's sett, the cave and other features not shown on the 25-inch map. They made notes of particular features that attracted their attention, including a monument which they later discovered was called Rodney's Pillar. The inevitable question: 'Who was Rodney?' led the group to Trafalgar, Admiral Rodney, and the popularity of local oak for the great warships of the day.

Before leaving the site I allowed the children to enter the cave in small groups and during each visit I persuaded them to extinguish their torches and to stand and listen quietly. I also sat the whole group down and drew their attention to near and distant features, the different farming land and other aspects that might generate enthusiasm in the study of the area.

On the way down the hill to the 'bus we heard the most distinctive song of a willow warbler but failed to see it. (During a later visit by a group we were fortunate in finding the nest.) It must have been a very early arrival and was another of the unforeseen events that subsequently led to a great deal of work, on this occasion the migration of birds.

In the afternoon, while the trip was still on the minds of the children, I allowed a general discussion to develop. Towards the end of the session I steered the conversation back to the visit each had made into the cave. I asked for words to describe the atmosphere; I asked them to close their eyes and imagine they were back in the cave, and then I asked them to record in prose or poetry their feelings when they were in the cave. Here are two examples:

Lloyd wrote:

> *Exploring the Caves*
> The sunshine was non-existent
> Water dripped from up above
> Slime covered the walls
> The long, dark tunnel onwards led.

Mark wrote:

> *The Cave*
> Dark
> Gloomy
> Dead is the cave.
> Slimy
> Slippery
> Damp is the cave.
> Muddy
> Stony
> Low is the cave.
> Drips
> Hollows
> Make the cave.
> Big
> Small
> Torches light the cave.
> Fear
> Overcomes you
> In the cave.

During the days immediately following the visit each group leader described to the remainder of the class their activities during the expedition. There was a general feeling that we should go along to the local museum to see the coins, bones and other relics discovered in the other cave. This presented no problem so along we went.

The following week the groups, with some assistance from me, decided on some lines they would like to follow. It would take too long to relate in detail the development of the work of each group. What pleased me was the way in which group work overlapped at various points.

The group dealing with Offa's Dyke drew their map of the route it followed and wrote letters to various organisations for information, including the Offa's Dyke Association. For the first time most of the children realised how near the Dyke was and so we became the owners of a number of photographs taken by the children, one showing how a modern road cut through the Dyke. All the photographs were mounted and simple captions placed alongside and on a large map we located the spots recorded on film. We visited three parts of the Dyke and walked along it for a short distance. Lady Luck was with me, for a few days later the press announced that a national organisation was reported to be interested in making a public path along the whole length. Going back to their map with renewed interest the children realised that many of the place names were in Welsh. For example, Knighton in Radnorshire was called Tref y Clawdd or Town on the Dyke. Place names were listed and we subsequently ended up with a simple Welsh-English place name dictionary.

The building of the Dyke intrigued most of the group. John, one of the pupils in another group, brought along an artist's impression of its construction. It was suggested that perhaps a simple form of pulley was used to remove soil and boulders. Experiments with pulleys was the natural outcome with the children offering their ideas of how man has, through the ages, made work much easier for himself.

Of course, there was the inevitable question as to who was Offa. This led to a study of the division of the country in Saxon days and how the children's own town had further developed at this time. It was discovered that Offa's Mint had been sited in present-day Kent and that he was part of the story of our coinage system. This fact proved the link between this particular group and the children dealing with the cave. They had made a study of coins of Roman origin and had started by referring to the twenty-six silver Roman Denarii dating back as far as 32 B C that had been found in the other cave. Two of the coins were dated A D 118, another A D 125, and a third A D 128. Whose likeness was on the coins? It was a short step to the reference books, Hadrian's Wall and Roman soldiers. Did the pile of stones on one of the coins refer to the Wall? Why was it built? How might the coins have come to be in the cave? All these questions we attempted to answer. One member of the group had lived in Australia and could tell us all about decimalisation, which gave an opportunity to examine foreign currencies. I produced a copper penny made in Anglesey towards the end of the 18th century when there was a shortage of silver. Amateur numismatists sprang up overnight and coin collecting became as popular as the collecting of fossils, stamps and other fashionable collectors' items.

By now the children were under the impression that their town was historically the most famous one in existence. Who was I to disillusion them? We drew a large map and on it located all the interesting sites in the area. The map was placed on a suitable sheet of timber and an electric torch bulb was put at each location. Simple circuits were then laid under the board and, on pressing the correct button, the position of the required site would light up.

The children, who had been given work cards to guide them, had brought back soil samples and they compared them with the samples taken from the spoil heaps of the limestone quarries. There were considerable discrepancies between these samples, and the conclusion was drawn that some rock and soil had been transported into the area probably to fill in the old shafts.

Specimens of slime found on the roof of the cave were examined under the microscope and compared with those from immediately outside the cave and from the perimeter of the hill.

Children, again using work cards I had prepared, made various tests on rock samples attempting to compare, identify and classify them. Vinegar was used to test for limestone, the most common rock on the hill. Experiments and findings I expected to be written up in an orderly manner. Later on all the samples were displayed and labelled in boxes covered with clear plastic.

During their examination of the rock samples the children had noticed that some contained crystals of different shapes. Using alum, sugar and salt they tried to grow their own crystals. After leaving a piece of string in an alum solution overnight they were delighted to find the following morning that crystals had formed. They repeated the experiment using a sugar solution but were disappointed to find that nothing apparently occurred. They increased the sugar content but to no avail. This puzzled them and they were very down-hearted. They had, by this time, taken the string out of the solution and were busy talking about the possible reasons for the failure. They were preparing to try the experiment for a third time when they noticed that since the string had been taken out of the solution and dried crystals had formed. They discussed what might happen with a salt solution and came to the conclusion that in order to obtain crystals the string would have to be removed from the liquid. I made sure that they proved their deductions. The crystals were examined under hand lenses and the resultant shapes were examined. The shapes were drawn and later patterns based on the shapes were designed and coloured. Models of the shapes were also made from thin card.

Parents, too, were sometimes involved, and on one occasion two children returned to school one week and informed me that they had been by car to see Rodney's Pillar that weekend. We returned to the hill a few times as a class during that term to check on certain facts relevant to various aspects of study going on, and we nearly always found something new to interest us. The girls were particularly interested in the transition of the countryside from spring to summer. The views were quite magnificent and even the boys were often ready to sit and just admire the surroundings. There were frequent visits to the hill by one group only, under supervision of course, and these visits were always profitable in providing data for follow-up work in the classroom (fig. 6).

Throughout the entire study I encouraged constant discussion between all concerned. Very often, intense interest on the part of a child was sufficient to allow that child to pursue a particular line of study but at the same time I always made certain that the control of the study remained with me.

I stressed the need for careful presentation of the work in all forms and each group had to be prepared to explain its work to the others. I believe my concern for these elements contributes towards the children's attitude for this type of work for they usually show a sense of pride in their achievement.

The class of fifteen children for which I am responsible is attached to the large Primary school in which the study entitled *The Cave* was carried out. My group, because of their academic records, are brought from far and near in order to receive the individual attention needed to improve their abilities. The age range of the class extends from eight to twelve years. These are the children who have found school life much more frustrating than the more able child and are often curious why they have been transferred to this school.

It was Dr Ballard who once wrote: 'It is easy for the brilliant boy to conceal his intelligence but difficult for the dunce to conceal his dullness'. With this quotation in mind, I make my approach to the slower child. I try to create a suitable background and setting for individual work and progress. It is essential that I cut my coat according to my cloth and work with each child as a separate individual realising his or her limitations and needs and gradually building up confidence.

It is everyday experiences and interests that can help to create an acceptable learning situation for children such as these. The classroom must be happy and full of opportunities to arouse lively curiosity. In his book *How Children Fail*, John Holt writes: 'Most children fail because they are afraid, bored and confused. . . . They are confused because most of the torrent of words that pours over them at school makes little or no sense; it flatly contradicts other things they have been told, and hardly ever has any relation to what they really know, to the rough model of reality they carry around in their minds.'

For less able pupils particularly, I believe that I must give much thought to the work to be attempted. The study has to be so selected that each child can contribute something worthwhile or else the whole thing becomes just a time user and so defeats the whole idea of investigatory work, namely, finding out for oneself. I must always be alert to the opportunities presented by unexpected occurrences that spark off the interest of these children. I must develop a mind flexible enough to cope with the shifting interests of the children. I must be fully aware of the goals I need to attain in educating children who lack the normal academic gifts but I must permit the enthusiasms of the children to influence my route in attaining my aims. This particular study tested my ability to cope with a situation that arose with little warning.

One morning two bulldozers appeared behind our classroom to demolish the World War Two air raid shelters in preparation for the building of our new school canteen. These great machines were of particular interest to the boys and they watched them at work from the classroom window. Two of the group were particularly knowledgeable about bulldozers and I allowed them to go outside to talk to the drivers. On their return they described the mechanical workings of the machines and gave the reasons why a firm level surface was necessary before building commenced. Three boys subsequently made a model of the scene. Other groups made booklets containing drawings of their own and illustrations taken from newspapers and magazines of building sites in their various stages, the mechanical aids used and the people to be seen at work. Many words, new to the children, began to appear as simple captions and sentences were written alongside the appropriate illustration. One group made a large diary and as new happenings took place they were entered, very often in picture form. Within two weeks a large excavation had appeared, providing us day by day with something new to talk about, to draw pictures of and to enter in the diary. At some time each day we left the classroom to visit the site and at all times the workmen recognised the needs of the children and were most tolerant and helpful.

With the permission of a most co-operative foreman, we collected samples from the various layers seen in the excavation. These were labelled and displayed on a table, together with the examples previously collected. We had, on a previous occasion, drawn simple plans of the classroom so the word 'plan' was familiar to most of the children. We took the opportunity of measuring the excavation using a measuring wheel, and back in the classroom we drew it to scale and talked about the reasons for making plans prior to building. On my suggestion some children measured again, this time using a normal pace and also a tape.

The completion of the excavation work seemed to be the signal for the delivery by lorry of a variety of different materials including sand, cement, timber, bricks, mortar blocks, tiles. How were these materials made? Where were they made? How were they brought to our town? These were some of the dozens of questions the children asked. Our friend, the foreman, was a mine of information and never seemed to tire, answering our queries with a patient and tolerant attitude. He gave us samples of the materials which we displayed in a variety of ways. These displays enabled us to add to our list of new words, each of which was printed on a card and placed with the appropriate sample.

One word which was constantly being used was the word 'transport'. It held all the potentiality I needed to extend the children's work away from the immediate vicinity of the school grounds and to give them experiences in the town itself. David told us that his father had worked at the now derelict railway station. He even went on and, in a typical child's way, explained why the station had closed. So many children were interested that we decided to pay a visit. Before leaving school I gave each child a thick piece of card and a pencil attached. On the card were headings such as STREET NAMES, ROAD SIGNS, etc, and I explained that I wanted them to collect the relevant information.

Off we went, stopping frequently for data to be written down. We crossed the railway bridge and went into the yard where several engines were still stored. For many of the pupils this was the first time they had seen a real railway engine. A considerable while later we moved a few yards to the site of the new car park. Only Gareth, who lived on a farm, knew that until recently this had been the site of the cattle market. They were torn between their interest in the automatic barriers at the entrance and Gareth's information about market days. In two's they counted the number of cars and car spaces available. Returning to school, it was encouraging to find several children, not usually enthusiastic about writing, asking me to spell words and ready to talk about things they had observed. One group made a model of the car park which involved them in simple measuring (fig. 7).

One direct result of the visit to the car park (the former cattle market) was an invitation from Gareth's parents to visit their farm. For this we hired a mini bus. We were met at the farm by Gareth's brother who explained the layout of the farm buildings. The children counted the numbers of pigs, calves, etc, and jotted down the results for later use (fig. 8). We watched a sheep dog respond to Welsh instructions and collected samples of wool. The girls were shown around the house and they noticed that its stone construction was quite different from the red brick houses from which most of them came. Nearby we saw the quarry from which the stone had come and one boy thought that perhaps the stone for the canteen came from there. I suggested that we find out on our return. A model of the farm was made and a frieze painted as a backcloth. The resulting display in the hall gave the whole class a much needed boost and encouraged them to take a pride in their work. Yvonne, who found school life quite frightening, gained a great deal of confidence on this occasion.

My suggestion that our friend the foreman be approached to discover the origin of the stone was accepted by three boys, and it unexpectedly renewed interest in the material being used to build the canteen. The drainage system was shown to one group, and they gave the rest of the class a sensible description of how it worked.

The valuable experience of talking with other people is important to these children but it is essential to give them guidance with the conversations they will have. I usually go over conversations with them, helping them to gain confidence and suggesting that there are some aspects one should not pry into.

Colourful books are essential and the book corner should be a very important part of the classroom. I have been encouraged when a child has gone to find out for herself. For example, when we discussed the canteen, Mary discovered in the reading corner a book that told her what cave men had eaten. Previously Mary had taken very little part in any class discussions but now she was able to tell us quite confidently of her findings. Brian, who was at one time classed ineducable, read the story *The Little Red Engine*, retold it in class and compared it with the bulldozers.

Some children still talked about the closed railway station so it was decided to round off the term with an excursion on one of the few narrow-gauge railways still in existence. (Only three pupils had ever travelled by train.) We drew a large colourful map which covered the area that we would visit and related this to our classroom map which showed the location of each child's home. The management of the railway arranged for the children to visit a signal box and the driver's cabin and even allowed us to stop and picnic at a suitable point beside a river on our return journey. Two students from a College of Education were most welcome on this occasion, for they involved themselves whole-heartedly and produced numerous pamphlets relating to the origin and working of the line. Items for classroom development and discussion, together with new words, were forthcoming as a result of this excursion.

One of the most important aspects of teaching children who are unfortunate enough not to have been endowed with high or even average ability is the necessity to help them to be aware of their surroundings and to give them confidence to live with society. This entails taking the children out and confronting them with new experiences as well as introducing them to people. Such a method must inevitably be based on my ability to take advantage of all situations as they present themselves. It might appear to the reader that four main topics emerged during this particular term, viz. the building of the canteen, the visit to to the derelict station and new car park, the visit to the farm, and lastly the excursion on the small-gauge railway. They were all connected in some way or other and offered experiences both familiar and new for the children. Throughout, they were kept busy, actively involved in everyday phenomena. I have been satisfied that the pride they have shown in their classroom and their willingness to show visitors their work meets my aims. Every one of the members of the class must be made to forget his earlier frustrations, usually caused by emotional instability and mental limitations. My interpretation of environmental studies, I feel, can help them to do this.

When Michael Flanders and Donald Swann recorded 'Mud, Mud, Glorious Mud' I am sure that they never envisaged that it would become the theme song for a study in a junior school. We had, only a few weeks before this study commenced, occupied a new open plan school during the 'rainy season' and we found that we were on an island in a sea of mud. This school replaced an old building that had originally been built for a village community of about 300 people. After the Second World War a large housing estate was developed in the area causing severe overcrowding in the original school.

Perched on a ridge between two valleys, most parts of the village offer fine views of the hills around. Nine kilometres to the south lies a rapidly developing market town. In spite of the relatively close proximity of this town, excursions for the children tend to be infrequent. The old village community has virtually disappeared and the area is still in a transitional stage and making attempts to attain some unified form. We have our share of deprived children, largely owing to the unsettled nature of the locality and its lack of amenities.

The school population consists of two hundred and sixty children between the ages of seven and eleven. One hundred of these, between the ages of nine and eleven, were allocated to a section of the school and supervised by three teachers of whom I was one. This particular section consisted of three 'home base' bays, a 'wet' area, a reference library area and a small science bay which could accommodate twelve children in comfort. Thirty-five of the pupils comprised my class.

For a number of years the school had attempted to use the environment as a basis for investigatory work. The switch from rigid subject instruction had not been an immediate decision but, with the removal of the eleven plus and greater emphasis on individual work, the whole school began to rethink its plans for the mode of instruction. It was at this time that the school was invited to participate in the official Environmental Studies Project. We did not accept it without much discussion: we tried to fix boundaries; we pondered on the need to give children a certain amount of basic knowledge, and we wondered if this new technique would satisfy our colleagues in the secondary school. Would it satisfy our need to develop creative skills in art and craft? Would it mean that language and mathematics would be neglected? Would it tend to become a one-sided affair with a teacher pursuing his or her own particular interests? These were some of the scores of questions we could not answer but we decided that we would become involved and evaluate the work as we proceeded.

Obviously, one has always to take into account the nature of the child one is teaching and looking back I now realise that when I began group investigatory work I underestimated my role. I had hoped that the children would acquire knowledge and know-how with little else but a few hints from me. I soon discovered that no direction meant a minimum of effort and few results. It was necessary to channel natural interests along specific lines. In brief, it was essential that I pre-planned. But here again I made a mistake. I pre-planned so much that studies became teacher centred and I frequently ended up as the only enthusiastic person in the class. My pre-planning failed because I planned not only the means but also the information that I wanted each child to acquire. I still frequently pre-plan but it usually takes the form of providing materials such as suitable reference books, apparatus, and assignment cards for slower and more unimaginative pupils, and creating simple situations that can act as stepping stones.

When we entered the palatial new school at the beginning of a new school year it had already been decided that, for the first term at least, each teacher would be responsible for his or her own class in most sectors of the curriculum. I did not know what general theme my class could pursue and, although it was the bane of our lives at that time, I had no idea that mud could prove useful. I complained to two children that they had walked straight from the mud outside across our well-polished floor. They denied this charge and proved to me that the mud on their shoes was not of the same colour by making further footmarks. In utter despair I said: 'Go outside and bring me several different kinds of earth, mud, soil or whatever you call it.' They did, and the subsequent study was born.

I suggested that they dried their samples in the kiln and I was immediately besieged with ice-cream containers, paper bags and even a lump of mud on a stick. I constructed a chart so that classification could take place on a colour basis (fig. 9). A few pupils thought they would compare the dried specimens with mud from their gardens. The results were compared and added to the chart. One boy found a lump of dry mud in a bag of Lincoln potatoes and he was delighted to discover that it compared in colour to the mud taken from the football field. Another lad whose football had been kicked into a local stream informed me that where the stream had cut into the ground one could see several different coloured layers. A subsequent visit led to a considerable amount of collecting of samples, experimenting with humus and eventually a display of the work. The lad from whom this phase had originated thought he was responsible for the whole major discovery and had one of very few moments of glory.

During these early stages there were days when interest tended to flag and I thought the study would die as quickly as it had been born but then something would happen and interest would be renewed. I saw a group of boys playing about with a spring balance and for a weight they were using a container of mud. It was decided that a sample of mud from the school grounds should be weighed, then dried and weighed again. We used grammes as our standard of measure and found the percentage of water in a large variety of samples. Again a large wall chart was used to record our findings.

At this time I was told by one pupil that one of the girls was 'messing about with the tumbler'. (This was a small electrically-driven tumbling machine we had purchased.) I found that she had put her dried mud and some pebbles into the container and was trying to grind it into powder. This process she could have carried out just as well by simply grinding the soil but at least it was an indication that the child was drawing some conclusions. We devised another chart and the results were classified thus:

(a) Weight of mud
(b) Percentage of dried mud
(c) Percentage of water in the mud
(d) Colour of the mud
(e) Texture of the mud.

I cannot help observing at this point that while I could see a number of useful skills relating to observation, classification, recording and displaying taking place, I was still concerned that the amount of factual information gained seemed smaller than by other methods of teaching. I was reminded by one visitor to the school that all the information the children had learned in nearly three weeks could have been told to them in a half-hour lesson. This remark did little to allay my feelings, but on balance I felt satisfied that the time had not been entirely wasted.

A comment by the headteacher in assembly one morning regarding the use of mud bricks in the construction of some eastern houses led to the making and baking of dozens of mud bricks. These were used to build a very realistic model of a Middle Eastern house. A considerable amount of written material on the people, their habits and the country in general filled their files, books and posters. While making the bricks we often forgot the time and the amount of heat required, which led to a variation of colour. The boys carried out a controlled experiment comparing the effect of heat on the colour of the baked bricks.

The study was gaining momentum. Five main groups were conducting experiments, searching for information and producing some interesting results. I was hard at it providing simple work cards and generally hovering about suggesting, guiding and sometimes directing operations.

One girl took a piece of hard clay and put it in the vice of the work bench and gave the handle a few turns. She said that she was trying to find out when it would crumble. Thus was our crumbling machine devised. On a circular piece of cardboard we marked the quarter, half, three-quarters and one full turn and fixed this alongside our vice. A range of specimens was submitted to pressure and the results graphed and interpreted. Another controlled experiment was undertaken in which a number of plants of the same species were grown in a variety of soils. Again the process was written up and findings recorded.

Powdered soils were used as colouring materials and the findings recorded. A group of girls put some of these particles under a microscope for examination. One boy remarked that if he scraped a stone with a sharp instrument he could get the same kind of particle. This led to a group carrying out some investigation on weathering agents.

Daily weather recordings using modern as well as home-made instruments had always been a feature of the old school and one of the first tasks was to erect the apparatus in the grounds of our new building. With the onset of autumn the effect of the weather on the grounds of the school was only too evident. These results were kept in prepared booklets and on weather graphs and maps.

To stimulate interest and to pacify my pre-planning urge I duplicated a small science work book which asked the children to undertake ten simple experiments on water and its effect on soil. The work was to be recorded under four headings:

(1) The experiment title
(2) What I did
(3) What happened
(4) What I have learned.

These work books proved invaluable as activities that some pupils could get on with when waiting for me to finish with another child or group. During an experiment one boy came up with the theory that clay is non-porous because the particles are so small they fit together too tightly to allow water to pass through.

As the days progressed so the time allocation to the study increased. I was not perturbed about this because there was an obviously increased involvement in recorded work, creative activity and a number of other essential aspects of a Junior school (fig. 10).

Their enquiries extended from the immediate surroundings as opportunities arose for discussion into the uses of mud in other lands and in other times. The group that had built the model of a Middle Eastern house not only enquired into the way of life of the peoples of that part of the world but devised their own alphabet and made mud tablets with examples of the symbols.

The theme of man's use of mud became quite evident as models of various dwellings showing the use of wattle and daub were made and other models of primitive mud huts. At the same time I expected the children responsible for these aspects to deal with them in some depth by exploring the world of the people who lived in these constructions.

A parallel theme at this time was how man had overcome the problem of mud. This led us on to roads and work developed showing how our modern highways had evolved from paths and tracks. An excellent replica of a section of Roman road was built by one group.

The rapid deterioration of the mud patch which comprised the grounds of our school led us to discuss that sort of area we might plan. A class of younger children in the next open area were very interested in what was going on and they designed and completed a large frieze using coloured paper, felt, paint, etc, that depicted their ideas of what the grounds should look like.

A second group with another teacher made a belt transect through part of the grounds. This they did by laying two parallel lines of string, two metres apart and twenty metres in length, incorporating a number of features such as stagnant water, running water, trees, rocks and a small marsh. Each member of the group was responsible for two square metres. The features observed on the ground were recorded on graph paper, and in the classroom a large composite of each child's effort was displayed on the wall. A novel way of recording was devised by embedding actual specimens of plants, stones and mud in a thin layer of plaster on compressed board. The belt transect was repeated in this way.

This recording of the area as it is and attempt to foresee its future inevitably led to the question of what it looked like in the past so we examined the 1842 Tithe Map of the area, the original Ordnance Survey map of 1887, and subsequent surveys which enabled us to see how the area had grown. The fact that houses were still being built allowed the children to appreciate that development was still going on.

One incident in particular comes to mind as an example of a moment of light relief. While I was out with a group of boys, one of them noticed a line of tracks which he followed, ending up on the wrong side of a farmer's fence. The farmer was nearby and one terrified boy soon lost no time in rejoining us. Explaining our intrusion led to a fascinating impromptu talk on what mud meant to the farmer. It gave us an opportunity of making many plaster casts of tracks which became one of the more spectacular aspects of the study, and also forged a link for the future with an interesting character.

Many of these experiences were expressed both orally and in written form. Language work involved using reference books, compiling scrap books, poetry writing and factual accounts of incidents and experiments. Mathematical experience increased, especially in graphical work. Possibly my greatest satisfaction came in the improved standard of careful observation, recording and interpretation. The study also allowed the class to work with different kinds of materials and in different media.

It is difficult to measure the success of such work but perhaps one child did sum up my feelings for me. He said: 'Sir, when I went home my mother said, "What are you playing around with mud for at your age?" but since I told her all about mud she hasn't complained.'

The Docks

Ham Lane

Figure 1.   The use of a vantage point
(see page 96)

Figure 2.   The do it yourself shop
(see page 15)

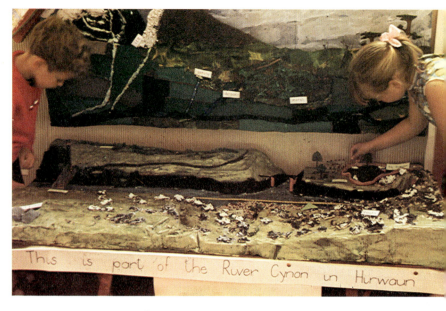

This is part of the River Cynon in Hirwaun

The River

Figure 3.   Model of section of the river (see page 24)

Figure 4.   Collection of stones from river (see page 24)

The Cave

Figure 6.   General view of the classroom (see page 52)

Figure 5.   At work on site (see page 47)

Figure 7. Modelling for these children was one form of
expression (see page 55)

Figure 8. Is that what a real pig looks like ? (see page 55)

Mud

Figure 9.   Classifying mixtures (see page 59)

Figure 10.   A busy classroom (see page 62)

Figure 11.   Listening to a taped
interview (see page 79)

Figure 12. Designing a road junction
(see page 80)

ure 13. ''Where is Buenos Aires?''
plate ready for shipment
e page 99)

ure 14. The technician from the
ber latex plant plays the role of
cher (see page 100)

Figure 15.   Recording by colour date of construction of houses
(see page 108)

Figure 16.   Recording by colour use of buildings (see page 108)

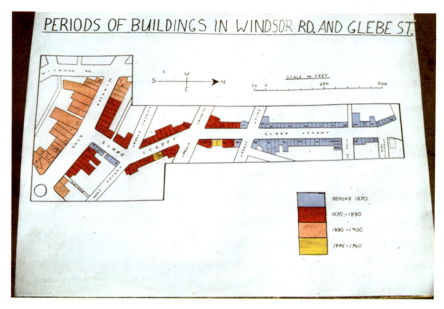

Much of the catchment area of the school in which I teach consists of large, late Victorian or Edwardian houses, many of which have been converted into flats. The well laid out streets are broad and tree-lined, giving an air of seclusion, yet within a short distance there is a trunk road and a very large and busy shopping area. Other features in the locality include a large park, the site of an old manor house and mill and an old parish church.

There were three hundred and eighty pupils on roll when this study took place. They were divided into eleven classes of which three catered for the 7–8-year-olds. These three classes had been organised according to age and the middle age group consisting of thirty-seven pupils was my responsibility. In 1967 I had returned to teaching after an absence of 12 years. For the first year I acted as a part-time teacher with responsibility for the basic subjects. In 1968 I became a full-time teacher and took charge of the class whose work is described here.

The brick and stone building is typical of the late Victorian era, box-like in design with high windows and ceiling. Four classrooms open on to a large hall, four others on to corridors and the remaining four comprise a small wing built in 1961. Four large obsolete cloakrooms have been converted into two library areas, one handicraft area and a small unit which caters for the less able pupils.

It was with a great deal of trepidation that I considered the problem of embarking upon a course of classroom practice that was rather alien to me after such a long absence from teaching. Would I be able to deal with the demands placed upon me in an approach of this nature? I felt that the choice of a suitable topic for study was crucial because every pupil in the class was a stranger to me, as I was to them. Hence it was essential that this barrier be removed as quickly as possible. This was feasible if all the children were able to contribute something. Consequently, I chose as a theme the children's homes and tried to envisage lines along which this could develop.

I quietly introduced the subject by asking the children about the types of homes in which they lived — terraced, semi-detached, detached, flat, bungalow; we talked about the types of houses they passed on the way to school, and the types found in the area.

The following day, after a discussion on what we were going

to see and a code of behaviour whilst on field work, I took the children on a short circular tour of the immediate locality following a pre-planned route that would give them a glimpse of the types of dwellings we had talked about. This expedition gave me an opportunity to draw their attention to the various building materials used in walls and roofs, shapes and types of windows, colour schemes of paintwork, types of guttering and downpipes, and so on. This tour provided even the most shy and reserved pupils with the opportunity of offering some small observation. Some children were delegated the task of counting the various types of dwellings. During the latter part of this brief visit we encountered a proud father who showed great interest in the work I was doing, or perhaps in his son's progress. I could cope with the children's questions, but an adult mind might have floored me. Not wanting to lose my self respect, I beat a hasty retreat.

Arriving back in the classroom we tabulated the results and divided the houses into the categories we had originally talked about and seen. Each child was now able to establish the type of house he or she lived in, noting the characteristics that might make it different from other houses.

Children drew, in personal scrapbooks, street scenes depicting the types we had observed, and we made model houses using brightly coloured gummed paper.

The gummed paper square was measured and the terms length and width were introduced. They found that the four sides were equal or the same. This was a good opportunity to introduce such terms as 'equal to', 'the same as', 'longer than', 'shorter than', etc. The properties of a square were ascertained and square objects in the classroom were pointed out and measured. A development of this was the listing of square objects found in the home. Some time was spent on estimating lengths and these were duly measured and the margin of error pointed out. Simple fractions were introduced as the paper had to be folded into halves and quarters for the models.

The models were now arranged according to type on a prepared base. The types of houses were tabulated and the number of children living in each type noted.

This was an opportunity to develop graphical representation from the pictorial method, as used in the infants' department, to the symbolic method. Each child was given a square of gummed paper which was to be his house. This was initialled and eventually stuck on a large wall graph. At this point some time was spent on graph spacing. Children had to ascertain for themselves the following facts:

(1) How many columns were needed along the horizontal axis?
(2) The colour needed for his particular type of house. (It had been previously pointed out that red squares, for example, were for terraced houses and green squares for detached houses. Thus it was realised that a key was necessary.)

Each child stuck his initialled square in the appropriate column and individual houses could be easily pinpointed.

The large wall chart entailed spacing along the horizontal axis only, so they were given a sheet of squared paper on which the actual number of terraced houses, etc, had to be inserted on the vertical axis. Emphasis was laid on the exact positioning of the numbers, especially the zero. If this can be established with younger children it should facilitate more advanced work in the upper classes. The graph was read and the children recorded their interpretations, e.g. twenty children live in terraced houses, etc.

Off we went again to study the houses in the immediate vicinity, equipped with a questionnaire which had been discussed prior to the visit. Our main interest was building materials and the craftsmen who used them. The houses in Agincourt Road were examined as these were typical of many streets in the area. The children showed no interest in the street names so I decided that the time was not ripe to deal with their derivations. The school, being brick built, provided an excellent example of the work done by a bricklayer, and the children were able to study the patterns and methods of laying bricks. Some bricks were brought in and we decided to build a miniature wall although I must confess that, having to work in such cramped surroundings, knocking down a wall would have perhaps produced more enthusiasm on my part. Each child wrote on 'My Home' and this was the beginning of written recordings. The results were very different from the old days of the weekly composition when half a page of badly written work was produced. Now they were writing as a result of first-hand experience and were using a wider vocabulary developed as a result of discussion following direct observations.

During this time one classroom and the head teacher's room had to be completely re-floored so they were able to follow up, step by step, the work involved. This led to the class examining the wooden parts, both outside and inside, and the children made lists of the work performed by the carpenter in their own homes. A collection of different timbers was made and mounted with the countries of origin shown on the map. The story of wood was traced from the builder's yard to the forest. The difference between wood for furniture and the wood used by builders was pointed out. The children made a list of furniture and found out what wood was used and its country of origin. Flags were placed on a large map of the world so that the children were able to check which countries supplied us with timber. A comparison between the map showing the timbers used by the house builder and that used by the furniture maker led to a simple comparison of hard and soft woods. A note was made of various roofing materials used in the neighbourhood and reasons for overlapping and pitch of roof discussed.

Plumbers, electricians, painters and decorators were investigated in relation to school and home. Reference books were in constant use at this time as some children searched for information. This led to a discussion on 'Do It Yourself' in the home. One of the girls surprised me — no, on second thoughts, it didn't surprise me — by saying, 'My mother says that she might as well *be* a widow for all the work my father does.' Being a practising feminist, I made certain that later work on paper hanging and men's work generally, was carried out by boys!

I encouraged the class to report on any building projects in the area and short visits were made to some sites within easy reach.

A piece of wool obtained from a barbed wire fence was combed and the fibres studied. Some boys attempted simple weaving on a cardboard loom while the girls knitted a doll with brightly coloured cotton. The pattern for the doll was a very simple one and well within their capabilities. They dressed the dolls with clothes made from old pieces of cloth. One boy, who at times was liable to distract others in the group, now insisted on learning how to knit. This he did and it was a blessing in disguise as at last I had found a way to keep him occupied. The story of wool was traced from the woollen mills of Yorkshire to the sheep farms of Australia. Silk and man-made fibres were also discussed. At frequent intervals the children pursuing a particular theme told the other groups of their findings.

They were encouraged to examine the labels on their clothing and find what material they were made of. These results were recorded. This provided an opportunity to develop their interest in colour and texture. A particular colour was chosen and the children brought along anything from fabrics to paints, and descriptive words such as shiny, dull, smooth, bright, heavy, hard, soft, etc, were used for each. It was most alarming to realise how difficult it was for a child of this age to describe an object accurately.

At this time the heating in school was poor, so it was no accident that one day the subject of heating was discussed and by question and answer we ascertained the type of heating used in each home, and a graph was drawn.

The children drew up a list of electrically-operated household equipment. This topic was now extended at their suggestion to include the study of electric circuits. I was a novice but managed to keep one step ahead of some of the boys while experiments were carried out with torch batteries and bulbs. A lighthouse was built and a simple electric circuit was set up. With the aid of a bulb holder the circuit could be broken and completed quite easily. Each child was given the opportunity to do this, thereby switching the light on and off. A simple model theatre was built with three footlights. Figures were made out of cardboard, and curtains were fitted.

This helped to fire their imagination and they brought in hand puppets. Simple situations were dramatised and we produced a musical play *Little Red Riding Hood*, to which we invited the lower school. This production was the highlight of the work so far. The excitement increased as they made their own costumes and scenery. The day for the production arrived and they even insisted on using make-up.

A few children built a larger house on a hardboard base. It was six feet long, four feet wide and five feet high, and was constructed in five sections which were slotted together to comprise two living rooms, a kitchenette, and a bathroom.

Each section was measured by the children and the work was allocated to various groups. The girls made the curtains, cushions, etc. This meant that they had to measure the windows and work out lengths and widths. They were very simply made and sellotaped to the wall. Another group made the cushions from odd bits of material brought from home. The boys, meanwhile, busied themselves with the carpeting and papering. One group of boys drew the designs for the living-room carpets, while the others completed the work on the kitchenette and bathroom. The most difficult task was the papering but the results were quite good and many of them had obviously watched their parents at work. The result would not have warranted a place in the Ideal Home Exhibition but it proved of great interest to the children. A simple plan of this house was drawn on squared paper, introducing the children to simple scale.

Throughout all these activities the children kept written accounts relating to their work and in some instances instructions on the lines of *How to dress a doll; How to make curtains*, etc. Slower pupils represented the activities pictorially, giving each effort simple captions.

Now was an opportunity, I felt, for the whole class to apply the exercise on scale to the classroom situation. I introduced this by getting the children to pinpoint various objects in the room and say whether a plan could be drawn the same size as the object or would have to be drawn to scale, as they had done with the model house. Each child was given a fairly large sheet of paper and by comparing this with the object they could immediately see whether it had to be drawn to scale or actual size. They drew plans of various objects in two ways:

(a) by drawing around the object, e.g. a book
(b) by actual measurement.

They could see that the larger objects would have to be drawn to scale but still retain the correct proportion and shape. Their scale models of cars and aeroplanes were extremely useful at this point.

Plans were drawn of various objects in the room, e.g. books, desks, blackboard. Then, of course, we attempted the room itself, always indicating the scale. A variety of measuring techniques were used ranging from a yard stick to a child's pace. The next stage was to get the children to measure selected rooms in their own homes, together with their contents. This provided a fund of information for scale plans to be drawn in the classroom.

It was evident that the children were prepared to go on drawing scale plans for the rest of the term. This did not quite suit me, but I realised that I could turn this situation to my advantage. I asked the children to draw a simple plan of their journey to school. The results ranged from single route lines to plan/picture three-dimensional attempts, i.e. attempts to include pictures of trees, houses, telephone boxes as part of the sketch maps. Naturally none were to scale. By discussion we came to the conclusion that we could not draw these to scale because we did not know the distances. This was the moment for me to produce the 50-inch Ordnance Survey map of the area and each member of the class was able to pinpoint his or her home and measure the distance from school, which in turn resulted in rough scale plans.

I gave them sheets of paper upon which only the school appeared. They were then taken out and a simple sketch map of the streets in the vicinity of the school was drawn. Trees, shops, telephone kiosks, were all marked for future reference when we returned to school to produce fair copies. During subsequent checking visits I was able to introduce the idea of orientation.

Each child in the class designed a birthday invitation card with the date, time and address on one side and a simple sketch map on the other. Accustomed as they were by now to right-hand and left-hand turns, it was possible to introduce compass directions. We correctly drew a large representation of the four points in chalk and I devised some simple exercises based upon children moving in various directions according to a number of paces. We talked about early explorers using the sun, moon and stars as pointers and from the Ordnance Survey maps of the area we discovered the directions in which streets ran, the directions the walls of the schools faced, and we kept records of the wind direction at a set time each day. Questions such as 'What is wind?' arose, and led to a number of simple experiments on the nature of air. For example, a balloon was fixed over the mouth of a lemonade bottle and placed on the radiator. The children were thus able to observe expansion and contraction, and I hope obtained some understanding of these terms.

I drew a large wall map of the area showing roads, shops, church, school, park and other features. The absence of names tested the children's ability to map read, assisted their powers of observation, and gave encouragement to those pupils who were slow in recording their findings by the written word.

Many other lines of investigation could have been followed at almost any stage of the work but in this initiation period I felt more comfortable in coping with a situation which was under control from my point of view.

The availability of suitable reference books for children of this age range is always a problem. I endeavoured, however, to use the ones available to train the children in extracting the relevant facts. Such training is essential for development at a later stage. I found that the children's enthusiasm was limited to briefer periods than that of older pupils, but at least it did not disturb the flow of interest.

Whilst group work was encouraged throughout the study, it was often convenient to work with the class as a unit, since I hoped that certain skills would be acquired by the end of the year. A reasonable amount of direction from me was necessary. Using this method I was able to place children in situations that might otherwise have proved less fruitful and interesting because of their lack of experience. One example of this was that in which we dealt with scale plans of various rooms based upon the exercise carried out using the classroom. In this way I made certain that every child in the class made some contribution, however small. The fact that the slower children found such difficulty in recording meant that a great deal of time had to be spent in this field. In my view, however, it was time well spent.

I found the work both stimulating and exhausting. Working in extremely cramped conditions did not help. There was little room for display and I feel sure that group work would have proved more successful had I had the space to move about. I feel it would be a mistake with this age group to delve too deeply into any topic — they thrive on new approaches, change of topic, varied presentation and working materials. In fact they are only as enthusiastic as the teacher. One of the weaknesses of the study as I operated it was perhaps the lack of involvement of the history of the area. This omission was deliberate. There were many occasions when this line of enquiry could have been pursued but I regarded this particular piece of work not only as a baptism for the pupils, but also for me. With the confidence I gained I can allow myself greater freedom in the future. In retrospect there are some aspects, perhaps, that I would have tackled differently, but I feel that I did at least profit by experience and begin to inculcate in the children the attitudes I regard as an essential part of education.

School Profile

The school at which this study was carried out was built in 1896. At that time it catered for the outer fringe of a city's population, but now the city itself has grown so that the school is surrounded by a large housing estate which caters in the main for professional workers.

The school building was typical of the late Victorian era, being rather dark and forbidding, but attempts had been made by the staff to brighten the warrenlike nature of the structure. (Two months after the completion of this study a major renovation of the school took place, which has transformed it.) The school yard contained the toilets in one corner, while the original main play area had been taken up by a block of three classrooms constructed of wood, extremely cramped and dark with no water facilities and little or no storage space.

This block housed 103 pupils, who formed the three classes in the age range 9 to 11 years. They were the group who were taught under a three teacher co-operative system. One teacher was responsible for mathematics, a second for language, and a third for environmental studies. Each of the three groups also had its class teacher who was responsible for music, physical education, etc. The remainder of the school consisted of four classes: two for the 7- to 8-year-olds and two for the 8- to 9-year-olds. These were housed in the main building. The staff, therefore, consisted of seven teachers plus a headteacher, with 236 children on roll.

The thirty-one pupils who conducted this study worked at it for a maximum of six hours per week, every morning until break, but where an overflow into language involvement or mathematics became very obvious there would be consultation between the three teachers.

The teacher who dealt with the work was a thirty-four year old man who had been experimenting in a quiet way with a variety of approaches for some five or six years and immediately prior to this particular piece of work he had attended a course run by the team of the Schools Council Environmental Studies Project. The pupils had been introduced to a more informal approach one year previously and were all, at the time this study was carried out, in the 10- to 11-year-old age group.

The Topic

The crossroads, which was the focal point of this study, was situated some forty yards from one of the boundary walls of the school. It was a dominant feature in the lives of all the children in the school; on the one hand it held all the terrors of the rush of modern transport and on the other its shops acted as a magnet to the children. The proximity of the area meant that many visits could be made with little or no trouble. I thought it could provide for an interesting and worthwhile study, yet allowing at the same time a sufficient degree of open endedness, a necessary element in any investigatory work. It could also provide features that would introduce geographical, historical and scientific aspects of study.

I could see the area as an opportunity for the children to deal with local aspects which would in turn lead them to direct links with other wider environments, through its shops, banks and traffic. I regard the interaction of children first with known adults and later, through interview techniques, with strangers, as a vital part of the linguisitic experience which should be provided by the school. Within the school there had been an attempt to familiarise the pupils with the locality from an early age. The area could provide for both factual and personal written accounts. Descriptions of such things as shops, people, events both past and present, and interviews came into the former category, while the area in its changing moods of sight and sound and sometimes smell provided the children with experiences which acted as the stimuli necessary for imaginative work.

All these factors influenced my choice of the topic and pre-supposed some knowledge of what an environmental studies approach should be not only in the classroom but in the wider context of the child's whole life in the school.

Progression of the Work

Although a great deal of individual and group work is desirable in an approach of this nature, in the initial stages class-organised exercises and expeditions are essential. I knew that I would require the class to use the 50-inch Ordnance Survey map on a preliminary visit to the crossroads and, as their experience in this field was limited, I did some mapping work with them. They drew classroom plans, plans of their bedrooms, gardens, etc, and we studied 50-inch, 25-inch and 6-inch maps of the locality. They learned how to use the compass and how to correctly orientate the maps.

For the first expedition I divided the entire class into pairs and gave each pair an enlarged section of the 50-inch Ordnance Survey map covering the area. This was placed on a piece of hardboard and held in place with a bulldog clip. It was agreed beforehand that shops would be marked with an S, banks with a B, traffic lights would be correctly marked, etc. The children were also asked to note anything of interest that appealed to them (no matter how apparently ridiculous). On returning to school, fair copies of these maps were prepared using a variety of keys; for example, the letters already mentioned and also colour. Classification of shops, banks, houses, etc, was presented graphically and interpretation was dealt with on a class basis. All these exercises built up necessary preliminary skills for group investigation of the same area. Considerable class discussion took place and was not always concerned with the more clinical details. In the general survey the children had discovered one minute house sandwiched between some large blocks of shops. It was apparently occupied by an elderly lady who was under some pressure to leave. Needless to say, in the discussion that followed on this social problem class sympathy came down heavily on the side of the occupant of the house.

The numerous points of interest noted by the children were now listed on the blackboard. These were discussed generally, and six of the most popular items were decided upon for group investigation. The six were chosen as democratically as possible, but I used some pressure when I thought it necessary. Again, as far as possible, a child was allowed to join the group of his/her choice. Group leaders were appointed and each group met in discussion to consider how best the theme could be developed. I spent some time with each group, suggesting and guiding so that the contribution of each group would give as much as possible to the whole study. Ideas were noted and the group leaders brought these to me. The results of these suggestions, together with my experience and knowledge of the children, now enabled me to prepare suggested 'lines of study' sheets. These laid down guide lines as to how the group could initiate its work but the end was left open to cater for the group's own development. The six groups now began their work on the following chosen themes:

(1) Roads
(2) Heraldry
(3) Traffic lights
(4) Development of the wheel
(5) People who pass by — people who passed by
(6) Various interests.

Development of Group Work

The group dealing with roads commenced by considering which roads met at the junction. They drew maps of the area and numbered the roads according to their official references. On a map of the region they indicated where the roads came from and they considered the main towns within a twenty-five mile radius through which the roads passed. They investigated the Ministry of Transport classification of roads system and drew their maps showing the routes followed by the main highways, and, in particular, the motorways, one of which ran close to the school. A comparison of the present route of the main road from London with that chosen by the Romans was made and extended into the future with an examination of the proposed motorway.

At this point a minute from the Parish records of 1799 relating to road repairs led to a study of the construction of roads. A great deal of information was obtained from the report of the Commissioners of Inquiry into the State of Roads, 1843. One boy, however, went off at a tangent and provided a good example of child research in reference books by dealing with the construction of Roman roads and other relevant data of that system. The lives of the famous 18th- and 19th-century road-builders were studied and the methods adopted by modern road construction gangs led to the study of roadbuilding machines. It was but a short step from here to the use of pulleys and levers, and I took the opportunity of suggesting this line of development to the group. An analysis of soil porosity and drainage was pursued which also involved road camber and guttering.

Side by side with the progression of the work, group folders were designed and constructed. Fair copies of work produced were placed in these and made available for other groups to read. Other copies were prepared for display on the walls of the classroom. My rôle in all this was to act as guide, moving from one group to another and attempting to anticipate the needs of the children. For example, I had to ensure that the necessary reference books were available. At other times I would halt the work and encourage a group to explain to the rest of the class the line it was developing. Frequently, there would be a need for me to give a group of children some practice in a particular aspect of their work. For example, there was always the problem of the less able children dealing with the use of reference books. This meant that I had to devote some time to assisting these children in overcoming this basic problem. Needless to say, not all were successful.

The enthusiasm of the children in their desire to join the group dealing with heraldry came as a surprise to me. The initial interest had stemmed from their observation of a large motif of a bird outside one of the banks at the crossroads; at least fifty per cent of the class opted for this group. A little persuasion on my part was necessary in order to 'convince' some that other interesting themes existed. The group began its work by arranging interviews with all the local bank managers. This was done by telephone and/or letter, which involved the children in learning an accepted procedure. There was some heart-searching as staffs of banks frantically contacted head offices for answers to the children's questions relating to the origin of the various establishments. It was shortly after these interviews that I realised that the group was dividing. One section was pursuing heraldry and the other the banking system of this country. If maximum interest was to be sustained then flexibility to allow this had to exist within my personal framework of class activity.

The heraldry section continued with a study of the origins and meanings of the city, county and other insignia. They designed a school emblem and heraldic terms became common in the vocabulary of this group. I frequently felt that their study was not broad enough but repeated suggestions that they should bring it to a close were repelled. It seemed obvious to me that these children were really involved. How they were studying was more important now than what they were studying.

The banking section seemed to have a broader approach. They progressed from the history of banking to consider security, types of locks and the work of security organisations. Some very interesting work on locks and keys developed and a considerable amount of useful material was sent to the children in answer to letters sent to various firms. The training of guard dogs brought the children into contact with hitherto unknown persons who were prepared to be interviewed. One of these, a representative of a national security force, turned out to be a responsive and sympathetic victim but retained the aura of mystery when he refused to answer certain questions relating to security.

The technique of interviewing was one which had been developed on previous occasions, and the children were aware that common courtesy prevented the posing of many questions. The same philosophy I attempted to develop when the children prepared written questionnaires. Most interviews were tape recorded on either a portable tape recorder for outdoor visits, or on a larger model used in the classroom. Naturally the children were trained to operate these (fig. 11). The tape recorder was also used extensively to record children's efforts in imaginative writing. I have already mentioned that another teacher was responsible for the main language section of the curriculum. The frequent discussions between this teacher and me kept him abreast of developments in the study, so that a visit to the crossroads would also serve as an experience in sound or movement that the children could re-live in their imaginations. A disused railway bridge at the end of one of the roads leading from the junction provided a theme for descriptive work in both prose and poetry. Imaginative descriptions of the crossroads in the future made a pleasant contrast to the factual accounts of the past and present. As the study progressed there was an increase in the number of aspects that could be dealt with by the language teacher.

Another group, which dealt with the traffic lights at the crossroads, examined the purpose of the lights. They observed the traffic at various times and in different weather conditions, recording their findings graphically. They timed the sequence of the lights and related this to traffic density in any direction. Suggestions and designs were made for a futuristic fly-over to overcome the traffic light problem. One child at this point very wisely observed that we should see what demolition would be necessary according to the 50-inch Ordnance Survey map. This was duly done and a comparative study of a similar type of fly-over a few hundred metres away began (fig. 12). Considerable class discussion took place on the social aspect of people being deprived of their homes. Progress seemed to be winning until some of the children realised that their homes might disappear in some future local developments. Contact with a firm responsible for maintaining traffic lights was made and the girls became particularly interested in constructing electrical circuits, together with the correct circuit plans.

One of the six groups had developed from a section of below average pupils. They were, academically speaking, the tail end of the class but although they could not sustain interest over a long period when dealing with a specific theme, nevertheless, they did sometimes enthuse over those aspects that caught their attention. It was natural that the 'lollipop' man (patrol crossing officer) should attract them. He was duly interviewed and proved to be a rare character indeed. A retired employee of British Rail, he had an appeal for these children and his stories of his boyhood as a cleaner and his ultimate promotion to driver helped me in stimulating this group to develop their aspect of the study. He it was who encouraged them to write for information to the Chief Constable, after showing them a cutting from the newspaper dealing with the shortage of suitable applicants for crossing officers.

Arriving at school early one morning, I discovered this group attempting to mix oil and water in an upturned dustbin lid. They were intrigued by the colours produced after seeing the patterns on oil spills at the crossroads on a wet day. From here they went on to discover where oil came from, how it was made and how it was brought to this country. Simple maps of oil tanker routes were drawn; murals of prehistoric mammals begin to fill their books as a result of discussions on fossils and their relationship with the formation of oil. Of all the groups, this one gave me perhaps most encouragement, for although the standard of their work fell short of that of the more intelligent pupils, it was gratifying to find such enthusiasm for work.

A further group dealt with the development of the wheel. They began by carrying out traffic counts with two, four, six, etc, wheeled vehicles passing through the crossroads. This data was graphed and interpreted. Friction experiments were undertaken and the development of the wheel throughout history was considered. This brought them to the modern industry with all its associated aspects, to design and road holding. A visit to a tyre firm introduced them to the meaning of the figures printed on the side. A range of models of wheeled vehicles from a Roman chariot to a heavy lorry was produced and these displayed, each in its own segments, in a large polystyrene spoked wheel. Some of the ideas for aspects to study came from me, while others came from the children as a result of discussions I held with them.

The final group was that which had originally intended to survey all the people, traffic, etc, that passed through the crossroads. Consequently, a detailed census of vehicles was begun based upon direction of flow, registration numbers, names of firms on lorries, types of vehicles, etc. All these statistics were graphed and interpretation attempted. The lights proved a boon to the children at this stage for even the slowest child could keep up with the help of the delays caused by the lights changing. Another important point was that little or no danger existed at the census points. The children were strictly forbidden to move away from the selected sites no matter for what reason. Questionnaires for street interviews of passers-by were prepared and these interviews undertaken with a tape recorder. I took this opportunity and guided the children towards the obvious question, what about the people who used to pass by? This led to a great deal of discussion into the crossroads of yesterday. The crossing patrolman already mentioned proved invaluable here. A copy of the 1875 Ordnance Survey 25-inch map was examined and a tracing of this superimposed upon the latest edition, showing clearly the developments. A model was prepared in which half showed the crossroads at present and the other half according to the 1875 map. Information was collected and displayed relating to the people and vehicles that would have passed by over the last two centuries. Using a commercially produced movable doll, the girls produced a series of Post Office uniforms covering the period of the postal service in this country. The designs for these were copied from illustrations taken from reference books and the girls were helped by an interested mother who came into school at frequent intervals.

As the work developed many aspects began to overflow from one group to another. As already indicated, there was a continuous interchange of information between the groups when prepared talks were given by each group. This slight pause also gave me a brief opportunity to consider how the whole was developing and a chance to make some provision for groups wherever necessary. The work continued over almost the whole term, that is, for ten weeks and was brought to a conclusion by finally completing the group books and making them available for all to see. One last activity was that each group outlined what it had achieved and was questioned by the remainder of the class. This was tape recorded.

Throughout the term I acted as a guide to the whole class, making myself available for discussion with each group. The success of the groups could not be measured just by the facts being assimilated; they were acquiring experiences and attitudes based upon their home area, which would 'serve in future study of other environments in time and space'. The children were learning to overcome the familiarity with their environment which often prevents their really observing it. After encouraging them to observe, I then required them to record neatly and succinctly in a variety of forms. The next stage was to teach them to interpret correctly and how to approach the interpretation on the basis of reason in relation to acquired facts. They had to be trained in how to interview, how to phrase questions and what questions not to ask. They had to acquire self-confidence in approaching adults politely and in a spirit of enquiry. They had to learn to work in groups, accepting the responsibility of leadership and learning to take instructions and suggestions from their own group leaders. All this, however, could not be acquired over-night.

As an experienced teacher whose approach was at one time extremely formal and who now regards himself as having moved through the transitional stage to one of a degree of informality, I am able to assess two differing approaches. The results outlined here I believe to be more advantageous to the children in the school in which I work than those arising from a strict subject basis in this section of the curriculum.

It was with many misgivings and no previous experience that I found myself introducing an Environmental Study approach in a large junior girls' school of two hundred and eighty pupils. The situation had arisen as a result of my attendance at a course which suggested ways of examining the environment at the primary level; ways which I must admit appealed to me.

I was responsible for a class of thirty 8–9-year-old girls in a school typical of the last century and scheduled for demolition. The school itself is surrounded by a number of interesting features, including a large car park, an automatic telephone exchange, a selection of old buildings erected over the past four hundred years, a castle which houses a local museum and, at the foot of the castle, a river meandering through a broad valley. The town dates back to Norman times and developed as a market town, a function it still retains. Roads lead from here in all directions and the valleys which these follow can, from the school, be seen radiating like the spokes of a wheel.

The school was well known in the district for its high standards of attainment among the pupils, but hitherto had never used the locality for first-hand investigation. I was plagued with the question that confronts so many people: would I be responsible for lowering school standards? Whatever the answer to this question was, I had committed myself to a new approach and had to begin somewhere.

The castle, being only a minute's walk away from the school, was to be our first outside venture. Consequently, early in the autumn term we walked the hundred metres or so to our chosen objective. I made no preparations for this visit, other than the normal chat about safety, for I wanted to test the children's reactions. Fortunately, it turned out to be extremely successful, for they were soon asking such questions as: why were the walls so thick? Who built the castle and why? We examined every part of the building and watched a master mason restoring part of one of the walls. We sat for a few moments in the sunshine and gazed down on the river and across the green fields to a modern highway with its rushing traffic. Back in the classroom we held a question and answer discussion on castles in general, and I realised that the children's interest warranted pursuing the topic. Consequently, I divided the class into five groups of six children for investigation and recording; I chose the groups largely on a friendship basis. I supplied each child with an individual folder, and each group with a 'Jumbo' book for displaying completed recordings. Although space in the room was very precious, I established a work table on which I put suitable reference books and an adequate supply of materials I felt could be used. I suggested that the groups should illustrate their first impressions of their visit in poetry and prose. Patricia, nearly nine years old, wrote:

> Castles of old
> Strange tales can be told
> It stands on the sweep by the green.
> Past battles were won
> With heroes unsung
> Now, only the ruin is seen.

Others wrote about the visit, the view from the castle, while others produced drawings and collage work illustrative of the building. A number decided to use the first person singular and imagine they were characters who had lived long ago. Ceri and Jayne, both eight-and-a-half, wrote:

On the battlements
I am a knight standing on the battlements. It is a dark and still night. I cannot see the stars very well, nor the moon. The water in the moat is black and still. I see something move. It looks like a man. I give the alarm! All the ladies and children are being kept in the Great Hall. The knights have taken their places on the battlements — we are ready for the attack.

Characters such as Norman maids and craftsmen all told their tales. Reference books and dictionaries were in constant use as the children searched for suitable words and phrases with their meanings. Cheryl had been impressed by dungeons, and almost brooded over them but she also produced this:

Thoughts of a dungeon prisoner
A lonely prisoner sat in a dark, dirty dungeon way beneath the ground. His thoughts were far away in the land he had left behind him. He thought of his wife and children anxiously awaiting his return. He thought of the stone house

where he was born. He thought of the many happy hours he had spent there when he was a child. He thought of the flowers and trees in his garden, and the birds singing there. Surely, that would be a very happy day when he saw them all again.

Although the school has a record of high standards in language usage, I felt that it was already livelier and richer in vocabulary as far as these young children were concerned and, above all, the work was relevant.

I was busier than any child at this period for, apart from circulating amongst the children, suggesting and encouraging them in their efforts, I was also preparing questionnaires and work cards for our second visit. This took place two weeks after the first. Working in groups they measured and drew rough plans and sketches of windows, doors, towers, etc. Specimens of plants growing in the walls were taken; photographs, not only of the castle, but views from the castle, were obtained.

One group began to make a comparison of the castle windows with those of the modern post office on the opposite side of the school. This was one point where I was able to assist, by indicating to them that it was possible to see other examples of the development of windows around our school; indeed, the school itself offered some examples.

Another group attempted to answer the question: who were the Normans? We were fortunate in obtaining some contemporary illustrative material at this time, for a national firm began to use the Bayeaux Tapestry as part of its advertising campaign. A considerable volume of work dealing with such aspects as routes from Normandy to South Wales, transport, dress and food now began to appear and final copy versions were placed in the group books. I was hard-pressed indeed to provide more reference books at this time and I made a resolve to rectify this shortage as soon as possible.

Until now there had been a distinct, if excusable, history bias to our work and I felt it was time to expand a little. With this in mind I planned a third visit to the castle to deal in greater depth with its position in relation to the physical features of the area. This I hoped would lead to the importance and function of the town today. With a little adroit manoeuvering on my part the study began to change direction so that hill farming, tourism, quarrying, communications and the development of the town as a dormitory area for industry became aspects of study. Common activities such as letter writing for information, collecting and interpreting of data in graphical form were comparatively easy at this stage. This was the point where I introduced them to sources such as the local tourist office, library and council chamber, together with a number of local factories. We sought details about the length of journeys to work from parents only in order to make it easier to collect the information.

As the weather was still extremely pleasant, I decided that we would visit a castle some ten kilometres distant, which was slightly larger than ours and in a better state of preservation. I was encouraged by their ability to recognise most features, and their use of the correct terms. Plans (free hand) were drawn, and on returning to school the least academic child in the class was the only one who incorporated the position of the castle well in her sketch. That made her day!

Imaginative writing still continued to flow from some of the children and Maria produced a poem entitled *My Dream*.

> When I look up in the sky
> I see three castles standing by
> Sturdy walls,
> Strong turrets
> When I look up in the sky.
>
> When I look up in the sky
> To see three castles standing by
> They are not there
> My castles in the sky.

From the river below the walls of the castle a few girls had brought to school some river-washed pebbles because 'they are the same colour as the stones in the castle'. I suggested making a mural of one side of the castle on a piece of hardboard four feet by three feet. Pebbles were collected from the river and these were stuck to the hardboard using Evostik. Raising this from the table so that it could be nailed to the wall involved the entire female staff. I wanted an apt quotation for the mural, and asked the children for help in finding one after first placing suitable books at their disposal. I was delighted to receive the suggestion: 'The splendour falls on castle walls'.

From this point onwards the topic took on a most unexpected and surprising slant. The children seemed obsessed with the stones. True, I had encouraged them to feel the smoothness and suggest words to describe the colour, texture and shape. Sharon had rarely, if ever, been known to produce anything creative, but shyly showed me the following one day:

> Stones are big
> Stones are small
> Stones are hard.
>
> Big and small
> Smooth and round
> Stones are hard
>
> Grains of sand
> Boulders tall
> Stones are hard.

Reference books told us about stone weapons and implements and the people who had made and used them. We brought this up to date by listing the people whose occupations bring them into close contact with stones in a variety of different forms, e.g. coal, slate, limestone, etc.

I introduced the children to the term geology and a number started to list local caves and collect rocks and fossils. One pupil's father was a mining engineer and he brought along a varied selection of fossils which most certainly contributed considerably to our display. Children (and parents too) became so interested that family outings were arranged for the sole purpose of collecting unusual rocks and pebbles, all of which we located on the map. As this is an all-girls school, I suppose it was inevitable that an above-average interest was shown in precious stones. Graphs showing the variety of stones in mothers' rings were made. It was no surprise that the diamond came first in order of popularity. From where did diamonds come? How were they formed? How were they cut? Back to the reference books went the children.

There was a spate of creative art at this stage; the girls poured out their instinctive love of beautiful things in the most colourful patterns and collages. There were models of sapphires, rubies and emeralds made from cellophane and festooned across the windows so that the sunlight could play tricks. A few had seen the Crown Jewels in the Tower of London, and these brought along some pictures and sketches. As the class was looking at them, one girl pointed to the Tower itself and remarked: 'I'm sure the Normans must have built that!' The circle was complete.

I am not prepared to say whether thirty girls and one teacher are better or worse as a result of the study we made. I am sure of one thing, however, that the classroom was an exciting and vital place to be in and that since that time I have striven to retain some part of the atmosphere that was generated. A good enough reason, I think, for being a teacher.

Environmental Studies and the Handicapped Child

From birth the pattern of human development progresses through a series of skills and activities involving the coming to terms with one's natural and artificial surroundings. A baby will investigate a new object by sight, touch and then taste, and so we learn by storing in a memory-bank the information received by our senses. We learn to select, discard and collect; we learn to regard certain objects as essential to our existence or comfort and that others should be avoided. A child grows into a changing world which has become bent, pushed or blasted into the shape in which Man, as the most intelligent of the animals, can survive most favourably – at least it is so for normal members of the species, physically able and reasonably endowed mentally.

The handicapped child, however, is a deprived child, starved of the experiences of the environment which others have had. This explains the difference in approach and methods of teaching adopted for handicapped children on the one hand and more normal children on the other. All children need to investigate and explore their surroundings: they must select and reject, see relationships and produce order from seemingly disorderly and often overpowering amounts of stimulii present. They need to discover the 'whys', the 'hows' and the 'wherefores' of life; the 'what' is frequently apparent, either actually or through television and radio.

Most experiences are 'natural' in that the experiences do not have to be presented in an artificial way. My neighbour's eighteen months old child runs into our lounge, grasps shiny objects, pushes and attempts to ride a tea-trolley; he dismantles everything before I attract his loving parents' attention away from the child long enough for me to deal with the situation. He gets blackened with coal, wet through and slimy from the fishpond, and scuffs his shoes from kicking tins. These are normal experiences denied to the child who lacks mobility. The handicapped child is beaten to it when a new experience is shared by others. He becomes a watcher, yearning for experiences which have been discarded at some earlier time by others. The less intelligent child, less socially and emotionally mature, and probably very clumsy, is also trying to gain these experiences at a later chronological age than that of his peers and is often ridiculed. The most usual defence mechanism is that of withdrawal so that social contact and even more physical experiences are denied.

Our tasks as educators are to help children *want* to discover, to feel the excitement of following the threads of related events and reaching conclusions which satisfy *them*, and to help them to acquire those skills which are necessary for this. The child must develop at his optimum rate. Remedial work is necessary for all subjects where a phase in development has been missed. Our job in schools for handicapped children involves remedial work in social and emotional development as well as in the academic. The physically handicapped child is 'at risk' towards withdrawal. He easily becomes the poor little cripple inviting and accepting pity and free ice-creams from all, numb to the world with its battery of external stimulii and bombardment of the senses. He must be made aware of his surroundings, enabled to cope with them to the best of his ability, and encouraged to be curious about his environment.

The school at which I work is modern and purpose-built, and the. children move as well as they are able in the bungalow building and along ramps to the flat, spacious grounds. More than 130 children from all over South Wales are accommodated, with the widest variety of physical handicaps and with I.Q.'s which range from below 50 to above 100. The age range of the children is from 5 years to the statutory 16 years, with one or two older ones awaiting further courses. The children are in their chronological age groups so that each class of fifteen or sixteen children has this broad band of physical and educational abilities. It is imperative that the work of each child is directly related to his abilities and needs. This requires a detailed know-ledge of each child, made easier by the fact that the school is residential and that vast amounts of medical, social and psycho-logical data are available to each teacher. The school is situated on the edge of a residential area of a town, near a city, docks, a beach and industrial centres, all easily accessible in our two purpose-built vehicles. The children are encouraged to progress further and further afield, and local evening and weekend trips are frequently arranged.

My class, Senior 1, consisted of sixteen children, thirteen boys and three girls, with ages of ten to twelve years. Seven children used wheelchairs permanently, three used them as aids to their walking, while only one pupil had normal walking ability. The I.Q. range was 54 to 103, the average being 78.

The children arrived after summer holidays full of the normal 'what we did' and I had decided that this class, mainly boys, might well show an interest in methods of transport. The children travel long distances regularly and see things which many normal children do on bicycles or by hiking. I contacted various helpful agencies, pointing out that they might be requested by the children for information. By a series of traffic observations, a roadside census, contact with the agencies, visits to and visits from the experts and all ensuing calculations and recording of information, we continued the project until satisfactory conclusions had been reached. Several points emerged:

(1) the class was new to me, not as individuals in our school community, but in the classroom set-up. This project outlined their abilities almost immediately

(2) grouping became natural, individuals requiring assistance usually seeking the help of the member of the class most willing and able to give it. This needed supervision to improve circulation by the children wherever possible

(3) the children began to have more realistic assessments of their potential abilities and their limited abilities in certain areas of knowledge.

Small, more individual projects followed in that first term. Some were successful, others less so, but the experiences involved were progressive, as were the necessary skills. The class had divided itself into three main social groups. They decided to collect information on air, sea and land transport, based on a survey of all travel undertaken by the pupils and staff of the school. Much of this work was successfully concluded, but replies from many agencies were often too tardy for the more eager members of the groups. With the approach of Christmas and its associated activities, the long-range possibilities of those particular schemes faded.

Studies during the following terms involved a thorough investigation of the class tropical aquarium during the bitterly cold winter months; a project on our newly-arrived mini-bus, from which the class's attention turned back to the aquarium, its specific qualities and our own making of glass; an extensive survey of the ground outside our classroom and the many natural and man-made objects found on it; a week spent on an exchange visit to our sister school in North Wales and exploring its environs; an excursion to the Science and Natural History Museums in London, and a week spent camping at the far end of the grounds of our school.

Skills gained in these studies have included letter-writing, formal and informal; the preparation of notes and diaries and their extension into full accounts; reading for information; measurement of length; the calculation of area, time, volume and weight; the preparation of graphs from surveys; map-readings and the use of survey materials; the making of aids for measurement, including a simple theodolite; the measurement and meaning of angles; some study of plants and birds; singing and tape-recording sound effects; speaking before an audience; a knowledge of the manufacture of glass and aluminium, and of slate quarrying; and some knowledge of the history of transport and of the public services supplied to our homes. Obviously, with such a wide range of capabilities, not all the children have a sound working knowledge of every aspect of every topic. However, by an examination of the progress of a representative sample of the children concerned in the studies, it has been possible to determine at least some of the values of the environmental studies approach.

Gareth is a ten-year-old suffering from spina bifida. He is able to walk awkwardly with the aid of elbow-crutches and calipers, but is most mobile in a wheelchair. Although he is of less than average intelligence he throws himself with zest into any job of cleaning, carrying or painting and is happiest when up to his armpits in water, dirt, oil or grease. He overcame most of the physical difficulties of the work and thoroughly enjoyed the practical aspects. He was more reluctant to record, but his use of written language was improved by his letter-writing and the recording of his experiments. The need to use reference books encouraged him to improve his limited reading ability.

Eifion is another spina bifida boy of ten who has marked visual perceptual problems and at the beginning of the year was a non-reader. After my consultation with the Remedial Reading Teacher, he was able to use pre-reading exercises as part of the project by selecting, collecting, cutting and placing pictures, copying and tracing works and using books to find illustrations.

These activities became useful and meaningful parts of projects, not a series of exercises *in vacuo*.

Betsan is a cerebral palsied girl with severe athetoid movements of all limbs. She has no speech, no control of her hand movements and is in the lower intelligence range. My problem was to evolve some way of including Betsan in the group. She began by producing a few simple signs to show her likes and dislikes of the details of a topic under discussion. Later, her interest was aroused to such an extent that she was determined to communicate by using artificial aids operated by her head or her nose to draw pictures and type her contribution to the project displays.

Walter is a boy who joined the class after a long term in hospital following an accident in which he fractured his spine. He is completely paralysed from the waist down and at that time he bitterly resented it. It was discovered that he was very interested in birds. He quickly became an accepted member of a group which included this aspect into its project.

Alwyn is a boy suffering from muscular dystrophy. He had reached the stage in his disease where he was permanently chair-bound and, like most muscular dystrophy boys of his age, was aware of the short span of life still left to him. His background was not a complete history of physical deprivation, for his had been a normal childhood up to the age of 5 or 6. He now needed an incentive to work for its intrinsic value and enjoyment. The projects provided the necessary impetus, but his arm and hand movements were extremely limited. He became the chief recorder of his group and carried out all detailed work for maps and illustrations.

Gareth, Eifion, Betsan, Walter, Alwyn and the remaining children were able to communicate freely with the others in their groups, adding their own contributions to each developmental stage. Most of these, like their fellow pupils in schools for the physically handicapped, spent some time in hospital and yet they were able to resume their places in their respective groups quite naturally. Individuals were more easily able to develop at their optimum pace and to follow their own interests provided that careful supervision by the teacher eliminated the possibility of severance from the main group.

In retrospect, it would appear that there are two seemingly

opposed methods of organising environmental studies: by teacher-motivation and by pupil-motivation. The former denotes a strictly prepared pattern of progress, the latter a rambling, unskilled movement from stimulus to stimulus. Somewhere between the two there lies a path of interest and gained skills towards an end-product which is seen to be purposeful to the child and to his supervising teacher.

The environmental study approach is suited to the handicapped child if placed within a framework of compensatory, developmental and progressive education. The whole child must be considered and the projects must satisfy specific needs and desires. He should be able to pursue an interest in order to gain knowledge and skills which can be applied to further enquiries. The teacher should goad, cajole, encourage and then supply information and teach skills, not imposing too many limited standards. The learning of the basic skills can be integrated into this environmental study approach or divorced from it at will. The whole programme must be meaningful to the child, then he will be helped to collect, select, reject and be alive to the wonders which surround us.

Environmental Studies in a Secondary Special Education Department

The Docks

The school in which I work is a new mixed comprehensive school which was opened in 1967. It is being built in two phases, only one of which has so far been completed. The school is on the outskirts of a large port which has extensive and varied industries. It is built on the fringe of a housing estate and is on high ground with panoramic views of the surrounding area. At the time of the study there were approximately 1,100 pupils. The school has a ten-form entry and the two lowest forms come under the aegis of the Special Education Department. At the present time, this department has four full-time members of staff, two of them (including the head of department) have extra qualifications for the work. The department is organised so that each member of staff is responsible for either a first- or second-year form for 21–22 periods per week. These forms are taught the basic subjects and the humanities by one member of staff. Each teacher is also responsible for teaching English and mathematics to either a third-year or fourth-year form. However, at the time this investigation was undertaken, the department was not fully staffed and some subjects, e.g. geography, were taken by the appropriate department teachers.

The form which became involved in the study was the ninth of the ten-form first year entry and it contained twelve boys and eight girls. The children had been selected for the remedial class on the basis of a number of criteria, including their performance in the 11+ survey, primary school and Schools Psychological Service recommendations, low reading ability, etc. Most of the class were in the I.Q. range 70–76; there were three who were recorded as non-assessable on the 11+ group test, and there were four pupils at the other end who were in the 76–80 I.Q. range. They were all at least three years retarded in reading, and a number of them were virtually non-readers. Some pupils had previously been receiving remedial treatment of various kinds and there was the usual sprinkling of behaviour problems. On the whole, however, the class was not difficult in the disciplinary sense.

In talking to the children I had been aware that their knowledge of their own area and of the town they lived in was extremely limited. They were unaware of the many places of interest which surrounded them and the knowledge they did have was garbled and inaccurate. I decided to use a double period, which had been timetabled as 'activity', to start a study which would attempt to give the pupils some information about their environment, encourage them to take an interest in their own town and improve their written and oral language. In order to gauge their interest I gave a preliminary lesson in which I attempted a brief outline of the growth of the town. We built up a simple map during the lesson and showed on it important landmarks such as the Guildhall, the rugby ground and the lido. I encouraged them to participate orally, which resulted in one boy asking if he could write about the local lifeboat as he had a relative who lived near the lifeboat station. At the end of the session it was decided to call the study *Our Town*. It was also agreed that the following week we should visit a well-known vantage point, a hill near the school. (fig. 1).

This visit took up a whole afternoon and the observation and investigation was divided into two parts: (i) What is on the hill? (ii) What can be seen from the hill — interesting landmarks, the docks, railway, main roads, etc? The hill is ideally situated as an observation point but it is also of interest itself. Simple outline maps of the hill and its immediate environs had been prepared beforehand and the children were able to record on them the site of such things as an old ruined windmill, a new television booster aerial, smallholdings and a small farm. Much of this recording consisted of symbols. Many questions arose quite naturally from this. Why was the windmill built in that position? How was the grain brought to the mill? Why was the television aerial built on the hilltop? It was also interesting to find out what crops were grown on the smallholdings and what stock was kept. Notes were made of the flora and fauna seen on the hill and heathers, grasses and other plants were collected. Later, a class map of the hill was made showing the main tracks and the sites of the mill and so on seen on the trip. From the hill one has a magnificent birds-eye view of the docks. Some sketches were made of the layout of the docks and of the shipping. The main interest of the children obviously lay with the docks, so I decided that this would be the topic for further study.

I had already received co-operation from a colleague in the geography department, who also taught this remedial form. He told me he was concerned about the limited amount of work

he could cover in the single weekly geography lesson he had
with this form so, after discussion, we decided to co-operate on
the docks study. By co-operating in this way, we felt he would
be utilising his time with them to the best advantage. As he was
also preparing a study with a first year fifth stream form we
decided it would be interesting to run both projects in parallel.
I was fortunate in being able to work in this way because my
colleague, being a geographer, could provide expertise in the
preparation of maps and diagrams and other necessary information, whilst I could give a broader, more general approach. I
could also use the flexibility of my timetable in order to correlate
our project with the other subjects I taught. It was fortunate
that our classrooms were opposite each other so that we were
able to consult quite easily about any problems which arose.
Perhaps the most important factor was that we were able to
work together without any clash of personalities or division of
interests.

As the project progressed it became apparent that we were
moving away from the wider aim I had at first envisaged and the
work now became more specifically directed at using the docks
as our centre of interest. I was quite happy about this because
there seemed to be so much that could develop from this topic.
We had decided that both the forms involved should visit the
docks together. We were also agreed that any visit must be well-
prepared and that the children should know what to look for
when we made the expedition. I felt this was particularly important with my own remedial form for I consider that in a learning
situation such as this a certain amount of structuring is necessary
if they are to gain the optimum benefit. With this end in mind
we prepared a number of cyclostyled sheets. Each sheet required
a certain amount of information which could be gained by
observation or by questioning. For example, one sheet contained
a table as follows:

Ship 1
(a) Name of ship _____
(b) Tonnage of ship _____
(c) Home port _____
(d) Country of origin_____
(e) Destination_____

(f) Ports visited en route _____
(g) Time taken from A - - - - - - - to destination _____
(h) Cargo:

Export	Import
Going to: Coming from:	Going to: Coming from:

(i) Flag on funnel or mast

Another sheet included line drawings of various types of ships likely to be seen at the docks. The pupils were required to identify the type of ship and include any information they could glean about it. For ease of recording, the sheets were stapled to a piece of stiff cardboard. Some time was spent familiarising the children with the vocabulary used and they were given guidance in the use of the recording sheets. As we were conscious of the inability of backward children to express themselves in writing, it was decided to take a battery-operated tape recorder with us so that first-hand impressions could be recorded, instead of being written up later. It was also intended to record interviews with any interesting people we should meet, and also to record the working sounds of the docks. In addition, a photographic record of the visit was to be made. The pupils were fully involved in the preparations for the visit. In English lessons we dealt with letter writing so that the bus company could be contacted and a quotation requested. When the quotation was received, the class then had to calculate the cost per head and decide if they would accept the quotation. A reply was then drafted giving details of times, date, etc. A letter was also written to the docks manager to obtain permission to make the visit. This point also led to a discussion on why it was necessary to prohibit people from wandering unsupervised around the docks. Some of the boys admitted that they had been swimming in the docks and had been chased away by dock policemen.

Our visit coincided with the opening of a new car ferry terminal at the docks so pictures and literature about this venture were collected in preparation. My colleague also arranged that a

technician at the rubber latex plant we were to visit would be
available to talk to the children about his work.

On the day of the visit we were fortunate in having fine
weather. We were also fortunate in having another member of
staff accompany us who had an excellent knowledge of the
docks and was thus an invaluable source of information. A map
of the route from school to the docks had been prepared beforehand and we stopped at various points en route in order to
record information about the journey. At the dock entrance there
is a Norwegian Church which is still used by the Norwegian
Community in the area. An explanation was given to the children
of how the Norwegians had settled in the town and reference
was made to the number of Norwegian names still connected
with shipping and its allied trades in the area.

Included in the recording pad was a map of the dock area
and as each stop was made the details were entered. The first
warehouse visited contained tinplate which had been made at
Velindre and was being exported to Buenos Aires (fig. 13). At
every opportunity, the appropriate vocabulary was introduced, e.g.
imports, exports, crates, bales, destination, etc. The tape recorder
was used to record conversations with workmen and also to
record the working noises in the shed. The dockers were extremely helpful and answered the children's questions very
readily. Two boys saw their fathers and it was interesting to see
how little the boys knew of the work done by them. There was
obviously very little communication between parents and
children about this aspect of their lives. They just knew that
their fathers 'worked on the docks'. Other children in the group
saw uncles and cousins at work, and this emphasised the point
that many of the docks' labour force live close to their place of
employment.

One important interview was recorded with a customs officer.
His intimate knowledge of the working of the docks and of the
shipping using the docks was of great interest. He was asked
about the tonnage of various ships, how often they visited the
port, and what were the colours of the various shipping lines. In
fact, he had to answer a great variety of questions and it was
interesting to see how eager were the children to ask them.
The children also asked him about his own work and this later
led to a quite extensive piece of follow-up work. We read of the

history of the Customs and Excise Service and of its present importance. Stories of smuggling were also collected. A number of seals used by Customs Officers for bonded goods were displayed, and information was collected about bonded warehouses and the types of goods stored in them. Other aspects of the work of a Customs Officer were also investigated and assignments prepared dealing with this topic.

As the tour progressed it became apparent that some of the children were beginning to appreciate the basic facts about world trade. They were actually seeing coal trucks on the coal hoist discharging their loads into a waiting vessel. They saw cars being exported which had the special exhaust systems and left-hand drive necessary for the American market. They could see the many products of local industries such as tinplate, oil lamps and toys being sent all over the world. At the same time they were made aware of our dependance on imports. There were ships discharging such diverse cargoes as barrels of wine, timber and cork. The cork being imported was destined for wine and brewery firms in the West Country, and this led to a later discussion on the need for good road and rail communications.

It was surprising that, although many of the group lived within walking distance of the docks, very few had any real knowledge of their operation. One boy, however, did know a great deal about the docks for he was in the Sea Scouts. This was previously unknown to me, but he was very proud of the fact that he could tell the group the names of the various docks. The working of the lock gates interested them very much. The principles of this operation had been described beforehand but seeing it happen made it real to them. They were also fascinated to visit the Communications Centre and hear the direct ship-to-shore contact between the operations staff and the pilot on board ship bringing the vessel into port.

The technician at the rubber latex plant was the father of one of the older pupils in the school and he proved to be most co-operative. He was used to having groups of visitors to the plant, and he had prepared what amounted to a lesson for the children. We were able to record his talk. His manner was very pleasant and the children enjoyed answering his questions (fig. 14).

The tour ended with a stop at the new Ferryport Terminal where the facilities for passengers, customs shed, restaurant and

so forth, were seen and then the bus took us to the far end of
the docks to see the docking facilities for oil tankers.

On our return to school, just before lunchtime, I was called
away to speak to a parent and another member of my department
supervised the class. She told me afterwards how impressed she
was by the excitement and interest of the children. They were
all anxious to tell her what they had seen on the visit and even
the quiet ones had something worthwhile to say. This was
particularly pleasing to me because the children's language
development was extremely poor and I welcomed any means
that would start them talking purposefully. This enthusiasm was
maintained during the period of follow-up work and proved a
most satisfying experience for all of us concerned.

The work which followed the visit was carried out at three
levels; by individual assignments, by group assignments, and by
class assignments. Each child made a folder in which he kept
his drawings, maps and written work. A selection of this individual
work was chosen for display in the classroom and care was taken
to exhibit it to its best advantage. Class maps were made of the
docks, the surrounding area and of the route taken for the
journey. A large flannelgraph map of the world was made and
the names of countries to which we saw goods being exported
were indicated. An extensive collection of photographs of the
docks and of the shipping using the port was also displayed.
The science department co-operated by helping the pupils to
identify the plants found on the original visit, and these were
mounted for display. They also prepared experiments to illustrate
the use of the plimsoll line.

The new car ferry proved to be an invaluable starting point
for correlated work. Newspaper reports and publicity handouts
were read in class and many items of information were gleaned.
Drawings were made of the ferry ship and the methods of loading
and unloading cars illustrated. The number of passengers and
vehicles was recorded and a great deal of mathematics dealing
with calculations of passenger fares, cost of berths, charges for
vehicles, kept us all busy. By using the timetable, the twenty-four
hour clock was introduced and individual work cards were made.
Those children who lived near the docks kept a record of arrivals
and departures of regular visitors to the port. Although it is now
over a year since this work was carried out, the interest has

persisted, and it is planned to take a large group of children from this department on the ferry for a weekend holiday in Ireland. When a group prepared a map showing the main rail and road routes to the docks, mention was made of the old canal system. It was decided to trace the route of the canal from its outlet at the docks to its source. This expedition was organised in conjunction with the head of the history department, who provided maps and other information. For part of the journey the group were able to walk along the old towpath and they were able to see a number of old work sites which still exist. It was pointed out how these works used the canal as a direct link with the docks. Mention was also made of a project which is attempting to restore the land devastated by former industries. Many of the children had taken part in tree planting operations connected with this project and so were familiar with its aims. Notes were made of the size and number of tunnels and bridges and the difficult lives of the old bargees were described. The group then travelled by bus to a point further up the valley where they saw old lock gates and the remains of old barges which are now submerged under the murky waters of the disused canal.

Although the work covered by this project was quite extensive, every attempt was made to maintain its simplicity. Children of such low ability as these would be discouraged if there were too many complications and we had to be prepared to discontinue with a subject if the children did not show the interest we expected. It was often necessary to give assistance with the simple research which was carried out, especially with the poorer readers. Where written instructions were prepared by staff the reading level of the pupils was taken into consideration. We also had to be prepared to accept, in many cases, small quantities of written work, for it was realised that this method would not suddenly change the pupils into literary giants. What was our concern was the fact that so many of them were attempting to express themselves in writing, as this, in itself, was an achievement. The staff who took part in the project are agreed that this is a very effective approach with slow-learning children. They maintained their interest and there was an improvement in their oral work for they discussed their visits and their assignments with far more than their usual fluency. They also gained a great deal of satisfaction from working together and seeing the end product of their efforts put on display. They were particularly pleased that we had a permanent record in the form of a series of coloured slides and some taped interviews.

The school in which this study was conducted became fully comprehensive in September 1970, but had been before that a large secondary modern school of 1,100 pupils with a nine-form entry.

It is situated on the edge of an extensive dormitory town which in turn is about three miles from a large port. The dormitory town itself was once a thriving port which developed as a direct result of the 19th-century South Wales coal trade. The former busy docks area is now overgrown with grass with the exception of a small outer dock used by pleasure craft. Ample evidence, however, is available for observation and as proof of the development and decay of one aspect of community in this locality. The residential area reflects the use of the local limestone for building the large residences of the shipping owners and the houses of the artisans. The streets are broad and well laid out, proving that even in the 19th century, industry did not necessarily have to destroy the amenities of an area. Post-1918 town development illustrates the variety of building materials that continually reflect 20th-century development.

It was decided by the heads of three departments, viz. history, geography and art and craft, that they would combine forces to introduce four classes of approximately 32 pupils each to an examination of the area. All these pupils were in the age range 11–12 years and the ability range of 30–60 percentile.

It had originally been the intention to include a fourth teacher, namely a natural scientist. This proved impractical, so consequently little scientific examination of the area took place. For administrative purposes the science periods were blocked with those of the three other subjects.

For some considerable time the heads of the departments concerned had expressed their dissatisfaction with the rare use of local features for comparison with other areas and as a result of deliberations, three aims were formulated:

(1) To develop in the pupils the ability to make close and careful observations, to stimulate enquiry and investigation, to promote the ability to abstract ideas from a variety of experiences of the environment. In short to attempt to get the children 'to learn how to learn'

(2) To enable pupils to become aware of the environment –

its continuity, the significance of its peoples' occupations, traditions and customs

(3) From personal and direct experiences of the locality to make the pupils aware of its associations with the wider setting in which it is placed and to compare and contrast the way of life in their area with that of other parts of the world.

To attain these aims needed a careful examination of the area itself to appraise what it had to offer and at the same time to incorporate into the study methods of working which could be applied to an examination of other areas.

The time-tabling of the study posed few problems. This was largely owing to the support given by the headteacher and also a number of teachers. The total time devoted to the four subjects of history, geography, art/craft and science for any one of the four involved classes had been 280 minutes per week. This was retained but adjusted into block sessions, as can be seen from this table showing the pattern over one month.

	Form	Monday (double lesson)	Tuesday (double lesson)	Friday (whole afternoon)
Week 1	1N1	Art/Craft	Science	History
	1N2	Science	Art/Craft	Geography
	1S1	Geography	History	Science
	1S2	History	Geography	Art/Craft
Week 2	1N1	History	Geography	Science
	1N2	Geography	History	Art/Craft
	1S1	Science	Art/Craft	History
	1S2	Art/Craft	Science	Geography
Week 3	1N1	Science	Art/Craft	Geography
	1N2	Art/Craft	Science	History
	1S1	History	Geography	Art/Craft
	1S2	Geography	History	Science
Week 4	1N1	Geography	History	Art/Craft
	1N2	History	Geography	Science
	1S1	Art/Craft	Science	Geography
	1S2	Science	Art/Craft	History

From this one can see that:

(1) Each subject specialist had eight periods of 35 minutes for environmental studies per week, split into sessions of 70 minutes, 70 minutes, and 140 minutes

(2) Each subject specialist could take each group on its own three weeks out of four

(3) Each class spent eight sessions for one week on environmental studies, six for two weeks, and four on the fourth week. The lack of science involvement accounted for this variation

(4) Blocking of the time-table in this manner allowed for interchange on the part of the children when it was felt necessary

(5) The large block of time on Friday afternoon allowed ample time for briefing for a visit, a visit itself and a little of the continuation work on arrival back in school.

The geography room is large, modern and purpose built, affording panoramic views inland. It has little, however, in the way of storage space for models and other relevant end products of such study work as is carried out.

The art and craft room is also large and is well equipped, but is lacking in storage space. The history room, on the other hand, is small, cramped, and is part of a portable building. These three rooms are some distance apart and although inter-change of pupils took place it sometimes made co-operation difficult. A large hall was occasionally vacant and was used for briefing prior to visits or for summarising results of visits, surveys, etc.

From the outset, the team of three teachers was aware that they had the advantage of being able to work together happily. They were familiar with the local environment, and young enough to withstand the rigours of field work.

The wide catchment area of the school brought together children from both rural and urban environments. A means had to be found to give each child an overall picture of what to many of them was a new area and at the same time to introduce many of the activities that would become part and parcel of the subsequent study. The answer was to take them on a bus tour of the area with a commentary and questionnaire designed for use during the stops for field work.

The trip proved successful and the majority of the children began to appreciate what was expected of them on field work and during the subsequent follow-up in the classroom.

It was decided to begin the main study in the town centre for the following reasons:

(1) It was within easy walking distance of the school
(2) There was shelter available during inclement weather
(3) There were clean conditions underfoot
(4) Information was easily available. (This is of paramount importance for young, inexperienced children.)

A cautious beginning would be made, using a common starting point which would allow integration of the three involved subjects.

The Scheme of Work

Phase I During the initial formal introductory sessions to class units each member of the team used his time in the following way:

(i) *Geography* To teach elementary mapping techniques which would be needed in all future studies based upon the development of the town
(ii) *Art/Craft* This teacher was concerned that his approach should not simply illustrate the work covered by the other subjects but that it should be illustrative of the creativity that could stem from aspects under study. For ease of availability the home of each child was used as a source of creative design
(iii) *History* It was decided to teach history backwards from two aspects:
  (a) A family tree study aimed primarily at showing the migration flow into the town
  (b) To show the pattern of change which has produced the modern town

Phase II This phase covered the following aspects of study:

(1) A simple analysis of the function of the town today as a dormitory for the city with the advantages of seaside residence

(2) A traffic census to show movements of traffic to and from the city on various routes covering a twelve-hour period every day of the week

(3) A more detailed study of traffic in the town centre to illustrate the present-day importance of the main road and shopping thoroughfare, in contrast to a side road leading to the closed docks, which was at one time the main shopping centre

(4) A questionnaire survey of both roads mentioned in No. 3 and designed to reveal:
   (i)   present uses of buildings
   (ii) former uses of buildings to introduce the concept of change
   (iii) dates of construction of buildings to show the concentric growth in relation to the docks (fig. 15)
   (iv) how buildings have been modernised
   (v)   the numbers of employees
   (vi) the home locations of employees
   (vii) how these employees commute

(5) Linked with items i–vii above, individual studies of various features seen within the street, e.g. styles of buildings, designs of shop frontages, patterns in stone and brickwork, building materials, window dressing, doors and locks, road signs, etc, etc.

(6) Mapping of survey figures to show:
   (i)   Present use of buildings (fig. 16)
   (ii) Dates of modernisation of buildings
   (iii) Dates of erection of buildings

(7) Maps, graphs and diagrams to illustrate:
   (i)   Where those working in the town centre live
   (ii) Where residents of the town work (based upon a survey sent to the parents of the children)

(8) An analysis and interpretation of the data obtained.

The survey then moved from the main thoroughfare to the former main road which led to the docks. Ample evidence in the street indicates the changed use of the property, e.g. shop frontages now curtained and converted to lounges; window canopies with their stanchions fixed to the wall, etc.

The development of the study through Phases I and II followed a pattern of enquiry. This was sufficiently flexible to allow for unexpected individual interests to be provided for. It involved:

(1) Discussions with class units prior to outside visits
(2) The preparation of questionnaires, task sheets and note sheets, and also the obtaining of relevant maps, surveying equipment, etc.
(3) The work on the site
(4) Follow-up sessions to collate the results obtained
(5) An analysis of results and class discussion on these.

The complete material resulting from field work covered such aspects as written work, graphs, maps, sketches, collages, paintings, pottery. Many of these were produced by groups of children as extensions to their individual files and sketch books. More than one pupil produced, among other things, excellent mounted collections of rocks and fossils, showing how individual studies could develop from class and group investigations.

A further record of work consisted of taped recordings synchronised to coloured slides. These were regarded as exercises in self-expression, as well as drawing together all the individual and group work.

The examination of the development and present-day function of the town involved the pupils in considerable experience in the use of Ordnance Survey maps, together with a comparison of these with old Estate and Tithe Commutation versions of the area. It was at this time that map reading introducing grid references, scale, direction and symbols was developed. Three-dimensional models of the locality were made from polystyrene. Photographs, both old and new, were collected together with aerial views; other sources included the records of public bodies, old town guides and newspapers.

The natural outward movement of the study having brought us to the end of the town's former main road, it was now an opportune time to move into what might be termed Phase III. It is worth mentioning at this point that the elevated position of the town offers excellent views of the derelict docks in the foreground, with the large city docks acting as a backcloth and allowing for excellent comparisons to be made. Three other important features were sited in the vicinity of the docks, namely:

(i)   A beach with a high cliff presenting an excellent example of the geological evolution of the area
(ii) The site of a Norman Manor house, now a farm
(iii) A church with connections in the region going back to the early days of Christianity.

Again plans were laid to visit and examine not only the former docks with its variety of light industries scattered throughout the complex, but also the beach, farm and church. Source material already mentioned was once again useful, and in this context a local newspaper was extremely valuable. A planned dig at a nearby medieval site which had roused the pupils enthusiasm had to be suddenly cancelled when a petrol firm stepped in and purchased the land. Numerous activities, including the construction and use of questionnaires, surveying and field sketching, were a few of the functions allocated to the pupils.

The three phases through which the study had moved had provided the pupils with two vital elements. First they had learned one way of examining a society and secondly they had had to interpret their findings in order that they might compare and contrast that society with others. This involved societies that had existed in the past and also those of the present day.

Thus the study began to depend less and less upon visits to sites, and more on using the evidence so far collated. The geography specialist was able to extend the children's use of the land utilisation map of the local farm by making a sample study of an East Anglian farm. A comparative study of a rural market town was carried out. In this case it was the town of Cheddar, as a result of having had in school for some time a stock of 'O' level examination maps of that locality. The same teacher later decided to take London as an example of a large urban study but the arrival of a student on teaching practice who preferred to study Birmingham meant a change of venue. As it happened, this proved fortuitous for it involved a number of aspects of study that linked that city with the local area.

On the historical side, very little political history was dealt with. The entire study was biased towards social and economic factors; moving back from the present and dealing with sections of historical time that were connected with the area: for example,

18th- and 16th-century smuggling and local characters; Norman manor houses and castles; the development of Church architecture; place names and their relationship to the invaders from the sea between AD 500 and 1000; evidence of Roman presence. This historical aspect could be summarised under four headings:

(1) Sources which offer evidence of events
(2) An examination of how an area developed within living memory
(3) How the area changed with each successive wave of people
(4) How other areas of Britain developed at the same time.

The department of art/craft provided the pupils with ample opportunities to express their observations of the area. Shop, hotel, garage and house frontages offered much in the way of appreciation of design, together with road signs. Many pupils became involved in the sketching of buildings erected in the last century from local limestone. The latter also offered a considerable number of fossils used for designs. Local clay was dug and provided a useful material not only for creative work in pottery but also to construct a range of prehistoric creatures connected with the geological formations of the exposed cliff face. A variety of models using a range of different materials offered further visual evidence of buildings and landforms.

The study was enjoyable and also successful, and continued over the whole of the first-year entry. This is not to suggest that there were no problems. In spite of considerable planning it was inevitable that the unforeseen was not catered for.

Finance on one or two occasions posed an embarrassment when transport was necessary and an allied problem was that of pupil teacher ratio on expeditions; one teacher per thirty pupils is rather high.

Movement of involved classes within the school would be much more fluid if members of the team and their classes could work in either purpose-built rooms or rooms which are in close proximity.

Time after time the natural curiosity of the pupils led them to scientific aspects in the locality but lack of expertise in this field prevented the team of teachers from making a sufficiently valuable contribution, and consequently a large aspect of relevant study had to be ignored.

At the secondary stage fixed sessions for this type of work are a necessary requirement. Unfortunately, since the weather cannot be controlled, outside excursions may have to be postponed, causing inevitable problems of continuity.

Finally, any teacher considering this type of work must be prepared to recognise that in the initial stages learning directly from the environment is slower than direct instruction, but it is based on firmer foundations. The aim is not simply to accumulate factual information about history or geography but to stimulate the pupils' interest and develop their techniques of finding and learning.

Using the Environment in a Rural
Comprehensive School

The school in which this piece of work was carried out is located in a large market town in the Welsh Borderland. The town itself is sited on the floor of the valley, which has always been one of the main routes for traffic between England and Wales. The surrounding hills, while of no great height, are often steep sided and in parts well wooded.

For centuries the town has served a very extensive rural district and today the school serves an equally extensive catchment area which includes villages and farms deep in the Welsh hills and along the borderland. On the western fringe of the catchment area the Welsh language predominates, but elsewhere English is chiefly spoken.

The school plays a vital part in the life of the community, providing secondary education for the majority of the children in its vicinity. There are approximately 800 pupils and 51 members of staff, several of whom are engaged in experimental projects. Its central position and the facilities which it offers have resulted in the school becoming the focal point for many cultural and sporting events for a very large area.

The school lies to the west of the town and despite recent urban expansion, a very lovely countryside is an important part of the environment. Some understanding of this environment is considered to be of especial importance as a preparation for adult life in this community. Many of the pupils will take the road into England but many more will remain in the area, and their number is likely to increase in the future as the town is now a development area. Although some industrial development is taking place, agriculture is still the basis of the economy and this is reflected in many of the pupil's interests.

For some time some of the staff of the geography department had felt that more use could be made of local phenomena and characteristics that might illustrate more clearly wider environments. The inception of the environmental studies project was opportune for the school at this time. Two ability groups were involved, with the head of the department acting as general co-ordinator of the work undertaken. In order to develop and illustrate principles and skills, the pupils were taken in coaches to locations within the catchment area of the school. These locations were free from dense crowds and traffic, no mean consideration with classes of thirty-five plus. A double period in the afternoon, with occasional overlap into the dinner hour, was allocated to this work. The aim of the study was two-fold:

(i) To acquire selected factual knowledge
(ii) To develop and practice certain skills and techniques.

The role of the teacher was envisaged as one of projecting the lesson from the immediate to a wider environment; from the descriptive to the conceptual stage; and of leading and channelling the children's interests and enthusiasm.

Six basic techniques were used throughout:

(i) Field sketching
(ii) Map making and reading
(iii) Observation and recording
(iv) The use of apparatus, e.g. compass, tape measure, weather recording equipment
(v) Question and answer — oral and written questionnaires/work sheets
(vi) Collecting and classifying of material.

At every stage of the work opportunities were grasped to compare and contrast the locality with other areas.

It became evident that the nature of the work necessitated an overlap into other subject fields if the children were to obtain maximum benefit. As a result of the interest shown by the history and science departments of the school an invitation was extended to them to participate in the study. This they readily accepted, and involved discussion and planning commenced immediately in preparation for year two of the pilot scheme. The timetable was constructed so that combined excursions used the subject periods which were arranged around the lunch breaks. Since the geography department had already gathered experience, it took the responsibility for selecting and co-ordinating the visits with the other subject specialists.

A combined visit was undertaken by the children to a fairly hilly but well-wooded area which held a wealth of material for investigation. The aim of the geographer was two-fold:

(i) To undertake a closed traverse to illustrate how maps are constructed (see diagram, p. 123)
(ii) To study the geography of slopes.

Preparatory investigation by the staff both as a team and individually is an essential feature of environmental studies and on this occasion proved to be, as it usually is, very enjoyable. The traverse had to be minutely planned and precisely timed, and as this was a completely new technique to the children they also had to do much preparation before the actual visit could take place. Field books were compiled and small practice routes were tried out in the school grounds until all had acquired a basic understanding of the technique.

The traverse was a closed one, divided into sections by major changes of direction. The work was carefully graded to enable the children to grasp the idea, for although they had practised in school, working in the field from a coach was new. The directions for each section, the mileage and the distance measured by timing were given but checked by the children. The driver greatly assisted by maintain a steady slow speed, possible because of the quiet country lanes. At first the children only had to follow and observe the information, then they added details of time, gradient and road surface, then the detail on either side of the road, and finally plotted the last section completely on their own. Working in pairs they quickly adjusted themselves to their new situation and with a little guidance from the teacher successfully completed the traverse.

Back in the classroom they had to decipher their coded books and begin plotting their traverse. The greatest difficulty lay in coping with the error encountered in closing the traverse but after this had been corrected they quickly developed the knack of plotting their information and some of the finished exercises were very impressive.

The more specific aims of the historian were to introduce the children to various kinds of historical records, architectural, pictorial and written, and to help them to perceive the close connection between such records and certain factors present in the environment with wider national issues and developments.

On the first visit the traverse was broken to allow the party to visit a village church. Each pupil used worksheets containing drawings of the building with questions following. In the class-room afterwards they studied copies of documents and in-scriptions and photographs. There was also much map work, written work and class discussion.

At the church, already introduced as a living symbol of faith through the ages, the children bustled around like small detectives, observing, discovering, recording, peering at a pre-Reformation memorial brass dated 1531, listing the many usages to which the valley oak had been put and asking questions. They were also attempting to answer questions such as:

Why did men choose to build upon this hillock?
Why did a village grow just here?
Why did they not build all the walls with the local shales?
From where did they carry the dolerites and sandstones?
Why does the tower carry only a wooden belfry?
Along which of the three river valleys did St Beuno probably come bringing Christianity to this valley?

The vicar, understanding the nature of this work, joined in, unobtrusively at first, but he became more involved later when he saw the children's interest in the unusual church organ.

A subsequent examination of excellent photographs of a brass rubbing of the priest on the memorial brass and of copies of the Latin inscription (given now in translation) led to work on church building and embellishment on the eve of the Reformation, the building of the tower of Wrexham Parish Church and a study of some of the oak screens for which the locality is renowned. A move outwards was made by work on the travels of St Beuno from Powys via Holywell to Clynnog.

The second visit took place a fortnight later. The route of the traverse was again followed but, while this gave the pupils a further opportunity of observing the area they had mapped, it was now only a minor part of their work. Preparation for the visit involved the building up of the vocabulary necessary to describe the landscape, e.g. undulating, valley floor, meander, confluence; to describe the land use, e.g. scrub land, gully erosion, exposure, soil creep, rock out-crops.

The children used work sheets which contained outlines of the landscape to be filled in by them. They referred to the relationship between the relief, settlement and communications. Back in the classroom the children wrote an essay entitled 'The Geography of Slopes', illustrating it with sketches from their field books.

The slope study led to a clarification of the variations and potential of land surfaces for agriculture. The higher and steeper slopes were defined as areas of difficulty and served as good reference points for the examination of other more extensive low potentiality areas throughout the world. Studies of tundra, taiga and deserts were made as extensions of the local conditions.

A lane which branched off the traverse route led to Gwestydd, a very beautiful half-timbered farm, standing high above the valley, the home of two of the pupils. Upon investigation, the farm house proved to hold a wealth of historical material and the lane itself, running from east to west, appealed to the scientist.

The building is a record of the 17th-century enrichment of the local small gentry families by the movement north of the wool trade from Pembrokeshire with its Flemish associations, of the local wool trade with the towns across the border, and of the infiltration of Puritanism from England into the secret valleys of the neighbourhood.

At this farm the children were again busy filling in the detail of the relatively simple Welsh style and the more elaborate English end. They roughed in the inscription which stands out boldly on the facade:

'O Lord my God in Thee have I put my trust. Save me from all them that persecute me and deliver me.

John Jones, Ad. Do. 1684.'

and wondered why John was afraid. They tried to answer questions such as: what materials were used to build this house? (Here were the timbers, below in the valley the oak was clearly visible.) Why could 17th-century families build higher and more elaborately than the 16th-century families?

From this site a very beautiful view was obtained of the small Welsh valleys unfolding in the direction of England, and the children saw in imagination the Welshmen weighed down by their wool packs as they trudged along to the markets of English towns and the surge of the cattle through this borderland out onto the midland plains. A great deal of study dealing with trade and social conditions over the last three centuries developed at this time.

A very brief visit to Pontyperchyll, another beautiful black-and-white house with Welsh and English ends brought an amusing story from the farmer about his farm and how it acquired its name 'Bridge of the Little Pigs', and there was much drawing of the Tudor Roses which decorate the 16th-century end.

Later the children made enquiries in the neighbourhood to find the probable meaning of place names, e.g, Tynybitfel, Gwestydd (Guest House). The answers, while amusing in their variety, failed to establish the firm connection with the drovers for which the teacher had hoped. Nevertheless, attempts were made to write Drover's Songs, e.g.:

> 'We are thirsty and weary
> We've been travelling all day
> Driving our cattle
> From Cardigan Bay.
>> *Refrain*
>> Heiptro ho, Heiptro ho,
>> Hurry you beasties, away we go.
>
> There's a bed for the night
> And a good glass of ale
> Food for the cattle
> At the inn in yon vale.
>> *Refrain*
>
> At last we reach London
> And our cattle we sell
> And we bring back gold sovereigns
> And stories to tell.
>> *Refrain*.'

The last line gave rise to much fruitful speculation.

Copies of two documents brought to school by the Jarman boys from Gwestydd were discussed and deductions made:

(i) An inventory of the goods of John Jones of Gwestydd who died intestate in 1686

(ii) A copy of the Will of Rees Jones of Gwestydd made in 1714.

The inventory revealed the abundant use of oak within Gwestydd and the girls were not slow in expressing their indignation upon finding that Grandchild Sarah Jones was to inherit only 'the smallest chest together with one guinea', while Grandson Gabriel was heir to all else.

Consideration of the inscription on Gwestydd, together with the study of a photograph of the ears of wheat from Cae'r Fendith (the field of the Puritan, Henry Williams, already visited on an earlier expedition) led on to the infiltration of Puritanism into the valley and along the range of hills upon which Gwestydd stands. Here the 17th-century gentry and the farmers in every known case had Puritan connections and even today the tendency to unorthodoxy in religion is marked in the district. The journey of Vavasor Powell to the valley from Radnorshire was mapped and the personality and work of Oliver Cromwell himself studied.

Perhaps as a result of a little self-indulgence on the part of the teacher, the work ended by taking an imaginary journey up the Cwm Nantcol and into the Rhinogs to Maesygarnedd, the home of another John Jones, the Welsh regicide.

On the day prior to the second visit the pupils had a short briefing period during the lunch hour with the science teacher. They were given work sheets and relevant information about the location and general purpose of the visit. The teacher wished to focus attention on the lane leading to Gwestydd, running from east to west and bordered with high hedges, in order to identify trees in winter using a key and to study the effect of aspect on the types of plants growing in the two hedgerows.

The children, following the Nuffield Science course in their main science lessons, had been using simple keys and now one of these was used to identify the commoner trees. Twigs of those which could not be identified in the field were taken back to the laboratory for further investigation. The children were encouraged to adopt a tree near to their home and to keep a record of all that happened to it throughout the year. They were also expected to collect and display in a chart the winter twig, leaves, flowers and fruit and to obtain a bark rubbing and any pictures of their chosen tree. This was a simple follow-up which Form I pupils could do with encouragement on their own without taking up class time. It gave them practice in observing and recording material which could later lead to useful discussion on methods of pollination and seed dispersal.

Someone noticed the 'green powdery substance' on one of

the trees. This was also taken back to the laboratory for further investigation: what was it? What did it look like under the microscope? Was it alive? Did it always appear on one side of the tree? If so, on which side and why? This was the bonus which had not been anticipated but which demanded investigation.

To study the effect of aspect on the types of plants growing in the two hedgerows the children had to draw a large sketch map of the lane and its junction with the main road. They located north and indicated it on their maps. Working in groups, each with a small section of the lane to study, they made a list of the plants growing in the two hedgerows, excluding trees, and recorded their frequency, so compiling a simplified belt transect. After this was completed, they were asked to note any differences and to suggest explanations.

Towards the end of the summer term a return visit was made to the lane to note again the differences in the type and frequency of the vegetation in the two hedgerows. This time a special study was made of the climbing plants which were classified according to their methods of climbing. Reasons for climbing were discussed and the pupils collected one specimen of each kind in order to write a brief, illustrated account. This gave them an opportunity of drawing a living specimen rather than copying from a book.

Collection of specimens was always strictly limited to those which were definitely needed. It is such a temptation for children to collect large numbers of specimens on the site only to discard them when, or even before, they return to school.

To operate such a scheme of work it is essential that there is the fullest co-operation between teachers as each must be prepared to give way on many points. The history and science staff left the final choice of a suitable location for study to the geographer, realising that if one is prepared to look hard at any area, it can be adapted to one's present needs. Indeed, once the work gets under way it frequently becomes obvious that the possibilities greatly exceed the time available for the study and thus time rather than paucity of material is the limiting factor. If a particular aspect requires fuller investigation a mini excursion may prove to be the solution.

The underlying aim of the team experiment was to work

towards an integration of the subjects involved, in order to present a fuller understanding of the environment. Integration can take different forms and it must be realised that it is not possible to achieve complete integration on all visits. Integration is a very slow process and the staff involved must work together for some time before this can be fully achieved. On this particular visit integration was based on a common area site which provided study material for all the subjects. Ideally a theme common to all subjects is looked for, but if one does not come readily it is better to abandon this idea. Another aspect of integration which can evolve as the staff work together is the use of specialist terms by the staff forming a common vocabulary across the band of study.

Wherever possible, the visit should be drawn to an end by one of the teachers giving a summing up. This is easiest to do when there is a common theme and again should not be forced in an unrealistic situation.

The staff feel assured of the value of this approach to teaching in the junior forms of the school as it does produce the maximum amount of both pupil and teacher involvement. The excursions arouse curiosity in the pupils and help them to appreciate the wealth of material that is readily available at hand. They provide them with training in the accurate observation, recording and analysing of material. The geographer finds that many aspects of the work have filtered into her more conventionally based lessons.

At first somewhat alarmed by the lack of chronological order in the choice of material, the historian now thinks that in a full two-year course with much 'to-ing' and 'fro-ing' over the centuries, some sense of sequence would be likely to rub off on to the pupils. Their lives gain through the added significance of the environment. There are, however, some dangers; a tendency to lose sight of the importance of personality in history – John Jones of Gwestydd, while arousing perhaps interest and speculation, must remain rather a faceless person compared with so towering a figure as that of Cromwell. Young teachers, perhaps new to the locality, may hesitate to undertake these studies because their knowledge is limited. This very limitation could be a good thing, necessitating a much more realistic exploration by both teacher and pupil, and preventing that flying away in too many directions at once which is a temptation to the keen local historian.

As the pupils were committed to following the Nuffield Science course the involvement of science in this work was limited to the biological aspect. When planning her work, the scientist was constantly seeking out the possibilities of link-up with the Nuffield Science course and this particular study greatly assisted the pupils who were studying 'The Variety of Living Things' (Nuffield Biology Book I). Variety could be observed in its natural state rather than in the artificial environment of the laboratory. It also served as a means of introducing the pupils to the ecological aspect of biology. However, under these particular circumstances the follow-up period was always too short. Sometimes the follow-up took place in the field, sometimes on the return coach journey or at the beginning of the next Nuffield Science session. The pupils were given homework exercises but much greater benefit could have been derived from these if more time had been available for supervision and general encouragement.

This work makes considerable demands upon the teachers involved, especially when it is being introduced into the school. Staff consultations take up much time, as also do the visits and the lessons. It is essential that the head teacher gives a project full support and that all the staff are aware of this, as sometimes it becomes necessary to encroach on their time and good will. It also demands energy and enthusiasm on the part of the staff — one colleague aptly described this work as 'A vigorous exercise, not a soft option'.

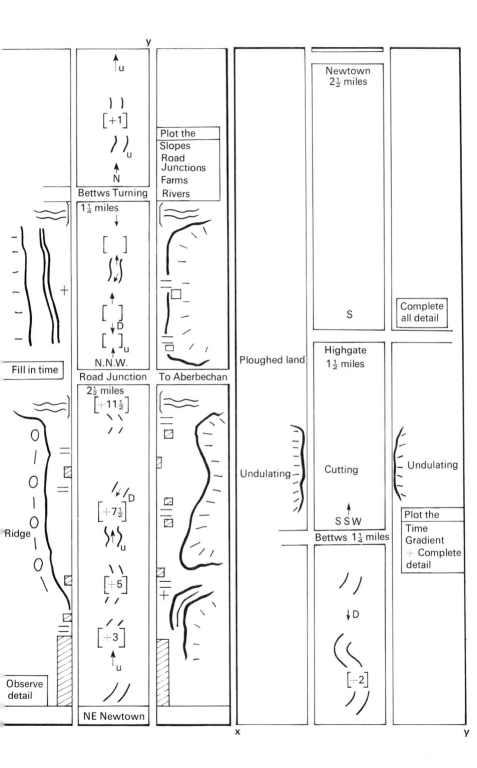